CONTENTS

GW00683453

"The Breathing Embodiment of Iron Will"

"Here he comes!"

The cry arose not from one or two but in concert from several of the dozens gathered in the windswept chill of the mid-March twilight on the eastern edge of Syracuse, New York. Lining a stretch of roadway at the foot of a hill where the pavement from the city turned into the dirt of the old Genesee Turnpike that went all the way to Albany, they bundled against a stiff wind. And they gazed eastward in the gathering dusk.

From the highway came the only sound that wasn't wind. Faint, very faint at first, it grew steadily louder. A relatively new sound, it was mechanical, the thrump-thrump-thrump of an automobile slowly headed their way. Edging into view, the car looked at first like an ant on the horizon as it steadily chugged through the mud and slop of the highway—followed by the faint figure of a man trudging steadily, a bit stubbornly, and seemingly in a hurry. Breasting a hill and drawing ever closer, the man's profile sharpened. He was clad in long pants tucked into knee-length leather boots and wore several layers of clothing. Atop his head was an oversized bushman's hat crushed on to white, silvery hair. Most revealing was his face: thickly mustached, it showed a man elderly in years who was tramping along at the pace of someone decades younger.

He was the reason everyone was here. He was close now, and

people were eyeing him clearly, prompting a mighty cheer from the crowd who quickly surged forward as he went by, threatening to engulf his route and requiring the lead car to clear a path to let the man through. With that, a blue-garbed cordon of Syracuse policemen, including Chief Martin Cadin, fell into step ahead of the man of the hour to escort him through the hubbub and onto the blessed pavement of the streets and into the city. Passing houses now, the man drew a steady rumbling of cheers from clumps of people gathered on front porches and street corners and leaning out of windows just to watch him go by. "Weston!" they shouted—ah, so that was his name—to which the old man would often turn and wave his big hat in acknowledgment while plowing ever onward, not stopping nor breaking stride.

It was a sight. A collection of people had gathered on the edge of the city during the cold evening of Monday, March 22, 1909, just to lay eyes on a man walking. Why such admiration for a man who was clearly just passing through? He couldn't have been a politician; they stop, shake hands, and give speeches. If he was some kind of athlete, he wasn't the kind you generally read about in the papers. That was the province of lithe, spry sportsmen of younger, far younger years, like the twenty-two-year-old Detroit Tigers' sensation Ty Cobb, who had just hit .324 in 1908 and won his second American League batting title; or the sensational boxer Jack Johnson, who less than three months ago had outlasted Tommy Burns to take the heavyweight crown. This craggy, white-haired gent with a walrus mustache who dressed as though he were on safari didn't fit the mold. This man Weston was *old*.

. . .

Striding through eastern Syracuse toward the middle of town, Weston kept his pace, still doffing his cap as policemen continued to lead the way. Now carrying a lantern to help him in the enveloping darkness, he headed from the Gene-see Turnpike to Forman Park and then down Jefferson and several side streets to Grace Will Congregational Church. Then, quite suddenly, he was finished, disappearing inside the church, where he went directly to a rear room for a rest. Weston deserved every blessed minute of peace; he had left Utica at five minutes past midnight and walked all the way to Syracuse, a total of fifty-six miles, in a single day—more than most of us walk in a year.

"Nothing of importance occurred on the road during the day," Weston said later, as if he had done little more than go the grocery store. But plenty had happened. Unable to sleep since 11:00 a.m. Sunday, Weston had rested that day and walked all Monday on those roads he described as "execrable." That was his way of saying his boots had sunk all day into the road's gooey red clay, making it impossible to establish firm footing and cover more than three miles per hour. "It was like muci-lage," Weston told friends that evening, "and whenever I pulled out a boot, it sounded like a cow's hoof coming out of the mud." Throw in a steady, strong wind, a painful leg injury causing him to limp in his last miles, and a prolonged lack of sleep.

But these were everyday challenges for seventy-year-old Edward Payson Weston. America's greatest walker, or pedes-trian, was in day seven of the most ambitious, audacious, and physically taxing feat of his long career. The day's walk to Syr-acuse meant he had covered 331 miles since starting the trip on his birthday, March 15, in New York City, for an average of more than 47 miles a day—slightly less than the 52-plus daily miles he averaged two years before on a walk from Portland, Maine, to Chicago. At an age when most were content to get their exercise by walking to the mailbox, Weston was in the midst of footing it some 3,900 miles from New York all the way to San Francisco and trying to get there in one hundred days. The day's wind and the "mucilage" of the road were typical of what he faced so far. Ahead was just about every other impediment imaginable, from mountains, snow, rain, sleet, intense heat, and mind-numbing cold to nasty dogs, menacing vagrants, aching body parts, as well as cars, those new contraptions that seemed to be filling up the roads.

But Weston had defied the odds for years. Walking, or "pedestrianism," was his profession, an unusual career he had launched nearly a half century ago in America by walking 478 miles in the dead of winter from Boston to Washington DC. Twenty-two at the time, Weston had walked, he said, as a penalty for losing a bet over the outcome of the 1860 presidential election won by Abraham Lincoln. As part of the payoff, Weston had to reach the U.S. Capitol in ten days and in time for Lincoln's inauguration, but he arrived a few hours late, bitterly disappointed that he had missed the ceremony. He made the most of things anyway—taking in the tail end of an inaugural ball and, some days later, meeting the new president himself. Along the way, Weston attracted enormous attention and then went underground for a time by serving as a Union spy, often reserving his espionage work—and walking—for the dead of night. And a legend was born.

On October 29, 1867, at age twenty-eight, Weston launched his professional walking career by accepting a challenge from a walking club in Maine to walk from Portland to Chicago—some 1,326 miles—in thirty days. Weston made it, even though he never walked on Sundays as a promise to his mother, and beat the deadline this time, by an hour and twenty minutes—taking home a purse of $10,000, a colossal amount for its day. In hindsight, walking was the easy part: Weston achieved his first big professional success amid rumors that he was in cahoots with New York gangsters on a massive betting scam. All along the route, he balanced a rollercoaster of extremes from death threats and atrocious weather to riots—yes, riots—over people trying to get close, as if he were a rock star. "Weston's name [became] a household word," *Harper's Weekly* wrote of the walk, "and really [gave] impetus to the pedestrian mania which [became] so general."

The popularity became so generalized because a pedestrian was the everyman of American sports—unlike jockeys or boxers, something that many spectators could only dream of doing, or participants in the growing mania of baseball, which many had yet to play. But who in the age before cars hadn't walked? And who hadn't at some point experienced the agony of swollen feet, blisters, or sore hamstrings from walking, say, four or five miles? Weston was at the forefront of this new breed of athletic hero, a marvel of endurance who, fortified by a prodigious, even freakish, ability to recover quickly, traipsed forty or fifty miles a day six times a week. Though Weston in his younger years often performed at tracks and county fairs, his cross-country feats wended by people's houses and shops, through neighborhoods and towns. From big cities to single-intersection hamlets, his presence was an *event*, one that brought farmers on wagons into town from the hinterlands. Today, the idea of watching a man walk by would seem to most to rival all the excitement of watching paint dry. But not in the late nineteenth and early twentieth centuries, when seeing Weston was a happening, an event to be remembered years later as the day the great pedestrian "came through here."

Weston was memorable in other ways. He was a dandy, a showman, and a colorful representative of his sport. Forever a friend to reporters, he had a host of catchy quotes and advice for healthy living at a time when many people actually saw little danger in smoking. Like many great athletes, Weston drew a multidimensional following, from men who wanted to be him to women who admired him and often attracted a courtly doff of the hat from the great pedestrian as he strolled by. Soon he wasn't just Edward Weston of New York City by way of Providence, Rhode Island, but commonly known solely as "Weston."

Looking to break time and distance records, Weston took on all comers and was soon touring America as an exhibitionist. Covering fifty miles in ten hours followed by a half mile backward to finish up and stretch out the muscles became a day's paycheck. When that wasn't enough for critics who thought he embellished his feats, Weston set out to prove them wrong: he walked one hundred miles indoors under test conditions and then became the first man to cover four hundred miles in five days as well as the first to walk five hundred miles inside six days. He accomplished what became known as the "magic 500" on a sawdust track in late 1874 at Newark Rink in New Jersey, eating on the move and catnapping as some bettors got behind him and others went against him. The wagering only intensified the interest; Weston finished under police guard, fearful of toughs dispatched by corrupt betting syndicates looking to inflict bodily harm.

Betting aside, most chose to sit back and admire the great pedestrian. In 1884 Weston was starting to carve a new chapter as the ageless one—journeying at age forty-five to Great Britain, where he wove a five-thousand-mile circumference around the island, prompting medics from the Royal Society to call it "the greatest recorded labor that any human being has ever undertaken without injury." Two years later, Weston covered 2,500 miles, walking twelve hours each day for five weeks— and trouncing his opponent, Daniel O'Leary, by *200* miles.

By himself against the clock or on a track full of competitors, Weston sometimes won and often lost. Winning was anything but automatic, which only endeared him to a public who rooted for him especially as he aged. When he failed, he tended to try and try again until he succeeded, earning a legion of admirers from Queen Victoria and P. T. Barnum to prominent writers, politicians, and all those people in small towns across America. Deluged with invitations to take part in parades and country fairs, Weston often did when the price was right. In an age before press agents and Twitter postings, the great man built a following by courting reporters and always making friends with policemen, barbers, railroad men, and hoteliers—anyone prone to help him along the way. That also went for veterans, particularly those, like Weston, who had served in the Civil War. It went for financiers, big shots, and presidents, several of whom Weston met. And it went for doctors, for whom Weston was a constant source of intrigue; they sought to examine him and take his pulse, many honoring him as a role model. Weston himself kept things simple. "I never was a fast walker—never tried to be," he said when asked about the secret to his success.

He knew himself well. Deliberate, adaptable, and able to keep going at an average speed of about four and a half miles per hour for surreal periods of time, Weston plodded onward at "a steady, even gait and stamina that withstood great fatigue," wrote his great-granddaughter, Joyce Litz. "Many surpassed his speed, but none could equal him for endurance." Wiry and compact, Weston was five feet seven; and though his weight would drop when he was in competition, he never topped an ounce above 150 pounds. He moved with a distinct gait, his toes turned out slightly in what he called his "flat-foot shuffle," not the more classical heel-to-toe style of most other competitive walkers of the era. He had his reasons: "Heel and toe will do for a time," Weston said, "but it ruins the heel."

Observers admired his unorthodox style, recognizing the way Weston seemed to amble as he moved, rhythmically swinging his shoulders. "You'll see a little man with white whiskers, carrying a short stick, and walking all over his body," a western railroad man said of Weston. "He'll be moving sort of slow. Yet take your eye off him and he'll be out of sight before you know it." Others, like New York reporter H. C. Long, focused on Weston's economy of motion. "It seemed as though he forged ahead as much through that swing as through his steady stride,"

Long said. "His head, his waist, his forearms, moved in harmony with the backward-forward throw of the shoulders and the forward-backward push of the legs."

Newspaper reporters couldn't get enough of Weston. He was great copy, always quotable and certain to sell papers—a wonder, an enigma, and a living legend rolled into one. That he outwalked everyone else on the planet as a young man was a given; that he still accomplished extraordinary things at age seventy was astonishing. "Moving freely and gracefully, despite a limping leg, eternal youth burning in his dark eyes . . . Edward Payson Weston walked on," the *Times* reported of his final miles from Utica to Syracuse. He was "a rebuke to senility, a triumphant foe of years, the breathing embodiment of iron will," the *Times* continued. And while Weston walked, he talked and spun tales to anyone within earshot. Oh, how he talked, holding forth declarations on what he did and why, the number of layers he was wearing that day, what he ate and drank. Weston's training techniques were precise and perhaps a tad eccentric. He started each day with a cold bath. After a long day of walking, he always rubbed his feet with whiskey, and he wore a red flannel nightshirt to bed as a preventative against rheumatism. Weston's feelings about footwear, his most important accoutrement, were just as pronounced. Wisely, he spared no expense with shoes—custom ordering his boots, which "ought to be made of fine French calfskin," he said. To wear or not to wear rubber shoes in the rain? Never, said Weston, convinced that wet feet absorbed excess moisture and triggered the tonsillitis that bugged him throughout his life.

Weston's diet was a constant source of fascination, written about and debated by newspapers decade after decade. The great walkist swore off pork but ate other meat and a lot of it—beef and mutton were his favorites. Weston also took to fish and fowl—boiled or roasted, never fried. He liked soup, especially in the winter, and never ate canned foods, though he recognized he needed a steady infusion of carbohydrates while walking. His favorites were pie, which he downed often and in large portions, and bread caked with butter. Weston also covered much of his food with pepper when available and feasted on fruits and vegetables. Dislikes were exotic dishes with sauces, which proved a particular problem in France. And he ate often, sometimes several times a day depending on how populated the place he happened to be and how far he still had to go.

All those miles gave Weston an acute and surprisingly modern understanding of the importance of taking in liquids. He drank two or three quarts of liquid each day—milk with an egg or two was a big favorite, as were hot or cold tea, lemonade, root beer, ginger beer, and sweet cider. Weston never smoked and used whiskey for his feet and "medicinal" purposes only. Hard liquor was out, and Weston swore that he had never taken a single drink at a barstool, a fact that endeared him to prohibitionists. For him, alcohol consumption was restricted to wine, Bass Ale, and Guinness, not American beer—he didn't like the taste.

No one ever counted just how much money Weston earned from pedestrianism. It was a lot, but America's greatest pedestrian was no businessman. For all the big purses he won, Weston had no steady profession for much of his life and often struggled to make ends meet. Considering himself an entrepreneur, Weston constantly invested in get-rich-quick ventures and moneymaking schemes that usually failed and left his family adrift and in financial peril. "The fact was, if he wanted to walk," said his great-granddaughter, Joyce Litz, "he had to find other ways to support his family, and he was a natural gambler." Some years, he and his family were flush with cash; other years were lean, with the uncertainty causing a constant state of anxiety for his wife, Maria, and their three children, forcing them to pinch pennies to make ends meet. But Weston barely noticed. "I feel much encouraged," he would say in a kind of diffident sarcasm of the family's fluctuating bank account. "Turkey one day and feathers the next." Weston wasn't being mean or abusive as a family man; mostly, he was an indifferent husband and father, choosing instead to focus on his walking. For Weston, his own comforts came first; feeling tired, he would sleep all day if he felt like it. "The condition of the whole man is basic to good health," he counseled. "Relax when you relax and work hard when you work and don't worry about keeping up with the Joneses."

. . .

Three hours after arriving at Grace Will Congregational Church in Syracuse, Edward Weston had revived quickly and felt chatty. Having delivered a lecture to an audience that filled the church, the old pedestrian was taken to a secluded corner of a restaurant on West Fayette Street for a late meal. George Ryan, an old friend from Syracuse, was there, among a wide assortment of acquaintances whom Weston had acquired in nearly a half century of roaming. So were several newspaper reporters, eager for a story and conversation.

"I ask for pardon for being so dopey," the great man said. "It's the wind. Fifty-five miles from Utica and the wind every step of the way. It makes you drowsy. Ah, how I'll sleep tonight!"

Getting the meal would help. Showing Weston the menu, his companions wondered what he wanted. "Vegetable soup?" Weston asked. "You bet. Is there anything like vegetable soup? It puts new life in you. Yes. And steak? Oh yes. I'm not very hungry, but I can eat some. I've eaten only six times today."

The order taken, Weston had a short piece of business, needing to file one of his first-person reports of his day, the 1909 equivalent of a blog. It would go to the *Times*, which was running the accounts daily.

"Would you kindly ask the waiter to bring me a few sheets of paper," he asked. "I've got to file my dispatch. Don't feel much like writing. I've got to wake up."

Weston was in luck. "Here's a newspaperman," a friend said. "He'll take down your dispatch for you. You dictate to him."

Weston was delighted and was reminded of just how much he relished the company of reporters. "God bless the newspaper boys, that's all I can say," he said. "One of 'em said to me in Chicago last year, 'Uncle, what can I do for you?' I said, 'Do for me? Good God! You've done everything for me already. What more can you do?' And they're all like that. They're on the square."

Stationery was delivered anyway. Pulling out a pencil, Weston said he would start the dispatch and dictate the rest. So he did, penning a few words before shading his eyes with his hand. But the endeavor was quickly forgotten as the soup arrived, which the great man devoured, chasing it with a welcome cup of coffee. And just like that, Weston seemed fully restored, a new man ready to hold court with tales from the road. "Beats all," he ruminated, "how often while I'm prowling along at night with my lantern, I'll hear some woman's voice from a dooryard: 'Mr. Weston, I saw you pass through here forty years ago and I was just seven years old. I shook hands with you.'"

"Did you?" Weston had replied. "Well, let's shake hands again, for I like to shake hands with a woman that'll own up to her honest age. God bless you, madam!"

The dispatch was completed, and the talk turned to Weston's impressions of the hamlet of Chittenango, some eight miles east of Syracuse, where the pedestrian had been that afternoon. "It's a good little place, but hang its barbers!" the pedestrian thundered. "They're robbers." Apparently, the barbers of Chittenango, where Weston had stopped for a shave, charged what he considered excessive rates. In most towns, the going rate was fifty cents, but not in Chittenango, where a barber had asked for one dollar, leaving Weston livid. "He got it [because] I never haggle," he said. "But his conscience ought to bother him more than his razor did me."

Weston got his steak. Digging in, the pedestrian kept talking, moving from tales of the barber of Chittenango to happier topics. "More people know me every trip," he said. "Many teamsters stopped their horses today coming from Utica through the mud, and sang out, 'How're you, Mr. Weston?' Make[s] a fellow feel good on a lonely road, hauling your hoofs out of the mucilage. Bless the people! I've tramped the country over many a time [and] they've been good to me. When you hear anyone hammering at human nature, he's a poor old grouch. He probably drinks too much."

No subject save politics was too big or small for Weston's commentary. He was sought for his opinions about many matters, to which he had ready definitive answers. Weston may have had it in for the barber in Chittenango, but he could barely contain his excitement about his meal in Kirkville, just east of Syracuse, where he had stopped at a restaurant for some eggs. "They were the best ever," said Weston. It was high praise indeed for a man who really liked his eggs. "I told my chauffeur here that if I ever heard of his running over a chicken, I'd kill him!"

Weston's appearances in sizable towns like Syracuse, Utica, and Troy, where he had just been two days before, were a big deal. But in the spring of 1909, in postage stamp–sized hamlets like Kirkland or Chittenango, Weston's stopping in for eggs or just walking down Main Street could be the biggest event in town in years. The following day, Weston would pass through microscopic Weedsport and pose for a snapshot that appeared to include sixty people, many of whom would presumably go to their graves with fond memories of the day they had seen and perhaps met the great Weston. How did they all happen to be there—and without Twitter to remind them? They read the papers, may have been using the telephone, and were expecting him. Miss it? No way.

On day seven of his great trip across the country, Weston

already had experienced a kaleidoscope of small-town America, all in New York State—while peppering his reports with praise worthy of a Hudson Valley travel brochure. That was Weston, usually effusive in his praise of the locals and endearing himself to one and all, not just a walkist but a one-man public relations brigade. Headed north from Tarrytown to Poughkeepsie, "the generous hospitality of the people hereabout [was] unbounded," Weston gushed. "At nearly every house I passed, the big-hearted women offered me tea, coffee, and eggs with milk." Stopping in Poughkeepsie, "that hospitable town," he enjoyed "a most excellent breakfast" at the Nelson House; chances are it had included eggs. The following day in Red Hook, Weston had been met by a drum and bugle corps, which serenaded and then escorted him to a local hotel. And that evening in Hudson, the chief of police, J. J. Lane, had met him at the outskirts of town and accompanied him the final few miles. The receptions had more than made up for what to date had been a challenging trip, already filled with enough snow, wind, and tough, muddy roads that Weston said were the worst—the absolute worst!—that he had ever encountered.

. . .

The hour was late, but Weston had an audience and was rolling now. "Say," he mused to his Syracuse friends, "you have towns through this section with some ungodly names."

"I came to a place today I understood at first to be called Swamproot. I understood later it was Wampsville. Even at that the name doesn't sound promising, but it's a good little town and I ate like a Christian there."

For all the loneliness of the long-distance walker, Weston relished his many encounters along the way. Excitable as a boy, he basked in the attention, remembered everything, and revealed an impish sense of humor. A friend reminded him of the story of the local woman who had told Weston she'd seen him walk through the area forty-five years ago. "Yes," said the old walker with a glint of mischief in his eye, "and the worst of it was that by her own admission, she tacked five more years to her age." That walk, he said, had been in 1869, not 1864. In fact, they were both off; it was in 1867.

But who cared that the dates were off? The stories were flowing, and Weston was heartened by the enthused receptions he had received in Troy and Schenectady, his fifth tramp through the region. "There's a warmer welcome for me each time," Weston said. "They're great people." Recalling another trek through upstate New York, he recounted a conversation with a small boy he had met west of Syracuse, near Point Byron.

Traveling in an open buggy, the boy spotted Weston walking. "Have a ride?" the boy asked Weston.

"Haven't any money," the pedestrian responded.

"Ah! Come on, it won't cost you nothing."

"Guess, I'll walk."

"How far you been walkin'?"

"Left Syracuse this morning."

"Why, that's twenty-seven miles! Where you walkin' to?"

"Oh, I thought I'd sort of stroll to Chicago."

"He looked wild-eyed at me a minute," Weston said, "then [he] grabbed the whip. 'I've struck a lunatic! Giddup!' [the boy shrieked]. And up the road, they went in a cloud of dust."

Weston had a storehouse of stories from a long and varied career. But dinner was done, and the old pedestrian was finally feeling the hour and all those miles of the day. Tomorrow, Tuesday, he hoped to reach Lyons, forty-seven miles away, and he was tired. Taking the cue, his chauffer rose: "Come, Uncle," he said. "You know you've got to be up by 5:00. Better turn in now." Weston didn't disagree. "All right," he said. "Good night, friends. Bless you all."

So with that, America's great pedestrian and one of its best athletes in the midst of perhaps his most ambitious walk of all turned to climb the stairs to a dormitory above the restaurant, where he would grab a few welcome hours of sleep. He needed it badly because for all the obstacles Weston had encountered in his first week, there would be plenty more—more mud, rain, wind, bad food, aching joints, weariness, and winds so extreme that at one point he would have to crawl forward on his hands and knees. All in all, the story of Weston's great walk west ranked as both a rolling national celebration and a stirring tale of triumph against the odds. It is one of America's greatest forgotten sports feats. This is how it happened.

Walk of Ages

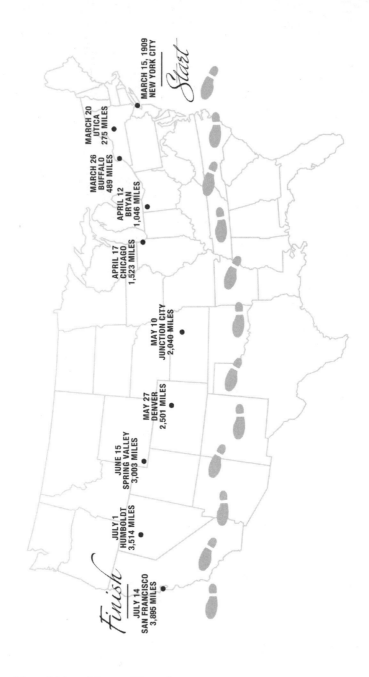

MARCH 15, 1909
NEW YORK CITY
Start

MARCH 20
UTICA
275 MILES

MARCH 26
BUFFALO
489 MILES

APRIL 12
BRYAN
1,046 MILES

APRIL 17
CHICAGO
1,523 MILES

MAY 10
JUNCTION CITY
2,040 MILES

MAY 27
DENVER
2,501 MILES

JUNE 15
SPRING VALLEY
3,003 MILES

JULY 1
HUMBOLDT
3,514 MILES

Finish
JULY 14
SAN FRANCISCO
3,895 MILES

Map of Edward Payson Weston's route

1

"Worried about the Outcome of This One"

The main door of the General Post Office at the intersection of Broadway and Park Row in New York City burst open, and in stepped a striking figure. He was an older man of a medium height with a white handlebar mustache who was dressed for either going on a hike or performing in an off-Broadway revue, or both. His long linen duster gave way to a lightweight blue coat and a shirt "of the colonial times," as one wrote. He wore riding trousers held up by a heavy leather belt and donned natty mouse-colored leggings and a sizable felt hat with a broad brim that an observer said "resembled a sombrero in all but color." On his feet were army boots. And he carried a cane.

On his seventieth birthday, Edward Payson Weston wasn't at the post office to mail a letter. He was going for a walk, a very long walk that he had decided to start in style, from the hallway of this handsome five-story granite building with the sloped green roof. It was March 15, 1909, in Lower Manhattan in New York City, and America's best-known pedestrian was preparing to leave for San Francisco on foot—ocean to ocean—looking to get there in one hundred "walking days," with Sundays off. Postmaster Edward Morgan and a number of other government officials had expected Weston shortly after 3:00 p.m., but the center of attention was nearly an hour late and anxious to get moving.

Weston would have to wait. Scads of his friends were there to wish him farewell, and Weston needed to bid adieu to as many of them as possible. First shaking hands with Postmaster Morgan, he moved to the rear of the post office, where some thirty of his Civil War–era comrades from the U.S. Army's Company B, Seventh Regiment, had assembled under the leadership of Captain James Schuyler. Together with the Metropolitan Band and a posse of mounted New York City police officers, they would escort Weston northward to Midtown Manhattan and beyond.

Their presence was needed. Dense crowds, drawn to witness the start of the great event, swarmed the surrounding streets. So great was the throng that Weston would be resorting to a standard bit of strategy he had learned from previous walks—using his friends as a shield from the multitudes, like linemen clearing the way for a running back, for safe passage through the clogged streets. It was in this festive air that a cheer went up as Weston strode through the main doors of the post office and back outside at around 4:15 p.m. Shedding his duster in the dry forty-one-degree temperature, unusually seasonable for mid-March in the northeastern United States, he bounded down the front steps of the big building, crossed Park Avenue, and was off.

Actually, Weston wasn't headed directly west right away—that would be through New Jersey—nor was he taking the shortest route. Instead, he would travel north through the heart of Manhattan and into the Bronx and then Westchester County. Walking parallel to the Hudson River, he would continue north some 175 miles, from his starting point all the way to Troy. Only then did he strike west through some of the bigger upstate New York towns of the Mohawk Valley, such as Utica, Syracuse, and Buffalo; the larger towns afforded the opportunity to earn a few extra dollars by lecturing. From Buffalo he planned to make another detour of sorts, meandering south through Olean and into Pennsylvania, before lurching west again, this time through central Ohio towns like Youngtown and Canton. Off the itinerary was Cleveland, where on his 1907 jaunt from Portland to Chicago, the police hadn't provided adequate protection from the surging crowds and a boy had stepped on his foot, wrenching his ankle. Gamely, Weston had soldiered on in pain and still reached Chicago.

On this trip, Weston planned to leave Chicago and head south again—this time sticking to post roads and the railroad lines through Joliet and Bloomington, Illinois, traveling nearly three hundred miles to St. Louis. The detour of several hundred miles, he said, was out of obligation to a couple of friends. From St. Louis, he would finally turn west for good, trekking another three hundred miles to Kansas City, and from there sticking to the Union Pacific rail line and planning to head into the heart of the West: Denver, Colorado; Cheyenne, Wyoming; and Ogden, Utah. Walking the rails was particularly hard slogging—the footing was uneven, forcing a pedestrian to move in a kind of diagonal, crisscrossing motion to maintain balance. But the railroad offered the shortest points between the remote settlements of the West; it could be a lifeline to supplies and even companionship.

From Ogden loomed one of the projected journey's most remote and barren stretches of all—the Great Salt Lake Desert and other areas throughout Utah and Nevada, where Weston wisely planned to walk the rails. In Utah he would switch to the San Pedro Railroad and Los Angeles and Salt Lake rail lines and traipse another 781 miles into Los Angeles. And from there Weston planned to turn north, traveling the Pacific Coast Road for the trip's last 475 miles into San Francisco. Walking nearly four thousand miles in one hundred days meant he would have to average forty miles a day—minus the Sundays. Age be dammed. For a man who had once trekked 125 miles in twenty-four hours, this was doable, even as a senior citizen, he said to himself.

The sheer magnitude and scope of the walk was dizzying. In a golden age of newspapers, of which there were many in New York, the seventy-year-old pedestrian commanded attention. That was particularly true in the *New York Times*, for which he would be preparing those short daily reports. For now, Weston was confined to the *Times'* sports pages, competing for space with spring-training reports from the city's three baseball teams: the Highlanders, or Yankees, of the American League and the Giants and the Brooklyn Superbas, later known as the Dodgers, of the National League. Closer to New York, the day's big news was considerable labor unrest among the six hundred or so Sicilian laborers kept away from their construction jobs at the U.S. Military Academy at West Point. The papers labeled it a strike, but the troubles sounded more like a lockout, imposed by academy officials who had charged that the laborers had offended military families by crowding them from sidewalks and fighting among themselves. Barred from the campus, the workers lodged protests with the War Department and the Italian ambassador, but they would never have their grievances effectively settled.

Edward Payson Weston's meandering route would afford both a drumbeat of steady newspaper attention and the likelihood of lecture income. In his nearly five decades as a pedestrian, Weston had developed a distinct set of rules for the road and a sense of rhythm and routine to his long-distance jaunts. He would rest on Sundays, a result of the promise he had made years ago to his deeply religious mother. And though he was being accompanied by a chauffeur and two trainers, Charles Hagen and S. W. Cassells, and was often trailed as well by a stream from nearby towns of reporters, children, and admiring locals, Weston was hypersensitive about venturing anywhere near an automobile while walking. Any contact with a car could set the critics to leveling those tired old charges that he was a cheat. So fearful was Weston of even a whiff of impropriety that he refused to hop on the floorboards of a car while conversing with its occupants.

Weston's team stocked the supply car with eggs, tea, bread, some meat, and plenty of ginger ale. They also carried ice as well as blankets, rain gear, extra shoes, and changes of clothing. Using a car marked a major change in Weston's long-time strategy of using horse-drawn carriages to haul his support group and supplies. Horses tended to wear out on long trips. And though Weston didn't like sharing the road with cars, friends had convinced him a car was certainly more reliable than a horse. In the end, the decision to take along a car was a no-brainer, enabling Weston's team to make a food run or to easily speed ahead to alert reporters of Weston's impending arrival and arrange a lecture or a hotel room for the evening.

Lecturing usually drew a crowd. Weston had been at it with great success since his five-thousand-mile trek in 1884 around England, where he spoke after each day's fifty-mile walk under the banner of the Church of England Temperance Society. Back home in the United States, Weston lectured for income. As a celebrity, Weston rarely needed lodging arrangements more than a day or two ahead, with no end of offers to put him up for a night and serve him a meal, both in the big cities and in the smallest of hamlets, too. So confident was Weston of finding a bed for the night that he carried no tent or camping equipment. Only when he reached desolate areas of Utah and Wyoming would it be difficult to find places to spend the evening. At least he could sleep in the car.

Those lonely days in the West were still ahead. For now, Weston headed in the most densely populated part of America—northward up New York's Broadway. Then he swung east on Twenty-Sixth Street and then north again on Fifth Avenue all the way to Fifty-Ninth Street, where most of his old army comrades, many of them tuckered out from the exertion, bade him farewell. By arrangement, three of the fitter men would accompany Weston all the way to Yonkers—Everett Brown and J. Chalmers along with a comrade from Company A, one C. A. J. Quackenbush, whose hefty name matched his girth. The thirty-one-year-old, 256-pound Quackenbush was perhaps the most accomplished sportsman of the three, a former U.S., English, and French weight lifting champion.

As a band struck up "Auld Lang Syne," Weston doffed his cap as a good-bye to his fellow veterans. Maintaining a steady trot, he lurched back west along Fifty-Ninth Street and turned north again on Broadway at Columbus Circle—a direction he would maintain all the way to Troy. Amid the cheers, some spectators jumped in beside or behind Weston but soon gave up. Few could keep pace; and every time someone broke in and joined the crowd, another seemed to drop out, in what resembled a fast-moving rugby scrum. Weston didn't let up for another three miles or so, until 125th Street in Harlem, where Hagen delivered a raw egg dunked in a hot cup of tea. The concoction pumped new vitality into the seventy-year-old athlete, who resumed his trek, crossing the Harlem River into Kingsbridge in the Bronx, then past Van Cortland Park, and across the city line. Though there were several miles left on day one of his great American walk, Weston had passed his first real test—the successful navigation of New York.

. . .

It was 9:15 p.m., five hours and some twenty-three miles into his walk across America, when Weston and his party reached the center of Yonkers, where he was due to lecture at the YMCA. As Weston wended up and down the rolling hills of Broadway, also called Route 9, the crowds grew from a smattering here and there to thick clumps filling both sides of the broad avenue as he neared downtown. By the time Weston reached the Y in the center of town, some two thousand people had streamed into Getty Square, hoping to catch a glimpse of the great pedestrian.

There was another immense crowd waiting for Weston inside the Y. The fortunate ones, they filled the seats and aisles to hear from the great man. Resting for fifteen minutes with a cup of tea, Weston bounded to his feet and headed into the auditorium, where John Brennan of the city's board of education introduced the pedestrian with a rousing "three good American cheers" to honor his birthday. Apparently, the cup of tea and the short rest worked—it usually did—and for the next forty minutes, Weston entertained the throng with his well-rehearsed talk on what he titled "The Vicissitudes of a Walker."

Charting those "vicissitudes" put Weston at the center of a time-honored American tradition of national sports figures who kept their names in the news by lecturing. The great baseball player–turned–sporting goods magnate Albert Spalding was one. So was former Yale football coach Walter Camp. Like Weston, both men had turned their celebrity into frequently quoted national spokesmen for the superiority of all things American. Spalding had been part of a one-sided commission that crackled to life after journalist Henry Chadwick dared to suggest that baseball had grown from the British sports of cricket and rounder. Of course it had, but Spalding wasn't listening. And so in 1905 he assembled a group to study the game's origins. "Our good old American game of baseball must have an American Dad," Spalding said. Three years later, the commission made its decision—declaring that baseball had been the invention of Civil War general Abner Doubleday, who was said to have organized the first game decades earlier in Cooperstown, New York. It was a wonderful story, but there was no evidence that the good general knew the difference between a baseball and a hockey puck. But discount the great Spalding? Some did; but for years, the story took hold, giving Spalding his blustery way.

Just waking up to the emerging commercial possibilities of using their names were baseball players like Christy Mathewson and Ty Cobb. Though a few years short of doing the vaudeville circuit, the twenty-two-year-old Cobb had just wrapped up a frantic winter of appearances here, there, and everywhere before heading to spring training. At the end of the 1908 season, Cobb and his fellow Detroit Tigers had each cleared $1,100 playing a series of exhibition games against the World Series champion Cubs. For a few more dollars, Cobb had jumped in—and won—pregame contests in the one-hundred-yard dash and circling the bases. Then, he was off to New York for a trip to North Carolina as the featured attraction of a motor caravan that promoted a "good roads" movement. Then, in New Orleans, he played in a weekend semipro league and refereed boxing matches. For Cobb, the pace suited him, a man as active in the off-season as he was on the base paths. What a rest he must have had at spring training in San Antonio.

Weston got right to it at the Yonkers YMCA, telling his audience he was walking to California to raise attention in the interests of stamping out "the Doctor Osler theory." He was referring to a controversial 1905 talk by the renowned Canadian physician Dr. William Osler, who had ruminated, possibly in jest, about the idea of a medical college where men would be required to retire at sixty-seven and spend a contemplative year before being "peacefully extinguished" by chloroform. Did he really suggest killing off the elderly? It stirred up a hornet's nest, the 1909 version of contemporary debates on assisted suicide and so-called death panels. "The effective, moving, vitalizing work of the world is done between the ages of 25 and 40," Osler theorized; and from then on, the invective had flowed. Osler's speech was big news in the popular press, which headlined their reports with "Osler recommends chloroform at 60."

How better to debunk Osler's theory than Exhibit A himself—the great pedestrian as he strode across the continent at age seventy. "What [Weston] has done is, as he intended it to be, a lesson in morality," the *Yonkers Statesman* wrote. "He has had the reputation, during a half-century of professional experience, of being honest in his athletic endeavors. His purpose has been ever larger than to show what can be honestly done with human muscle. He has set himself to emphasize the importance of temperance in continuing physical power and activity."

In his talk, Weston advised one and all never to use tobacco and to drink only in moderation. Plunging into the vast storehouse of anecdotes from his long career, he spliced some funny ones with the tale of how he had discovered the joys of walking—as a boy seeking a cure for partial paralysis brought on by rheumatism. Weston urged everyone to adopt a healthy lifestyle and, well, to get walking. And he reserved a special and particularly stern message for boys, who he said should avoid marathon running, which had been popularized in the dozen years or so since the first modern Olympic Games and since then at the Boston Marathon.

While Weston debunked the theories of Dr. Osler, he positively loathed marathons. They were destructive to young people, he said, leaving aside the fact that coverage of running events hijacked headlines from his own feats of endurance. At the same time he was speaking in Yonkers, two of the marathon's biggest names, the American Johnny Hayes from New York City and Italy's Dorando Pietri, were dueling in a highly publicized match race in front of a crowd of eight thousand at Madison Square Garden. The next day's *New York Times* would lead its main sports page with the Hayes-Pietri contest featured on the top left, columns one and two, pushing the story of Weston's first day to column three. For the record, Pietri won in two hours and forty-four minutes, a reversal of their legendary dual the previous July on a sweltering day at the Olympic Games in London.

The 1908 Olympic duel would long be remembered. It was

there that the marathon route was lengthened from varying distances of 24 or 25 miles to its standard 26.2 miles, created with a request from King Edward VII and Queen Alexandra that the Olympic Marathon start at Windsor Castle so the royal family could watch. That marked 26 miles to the stadium with organizers tacking on the final 0.2 mile, or 385 yards, at the end of the race so the runners could round the stadium track and finish in front of the Royal Box. That extra 0.2 mile would result in the most dramatic marathon finish in history, cementing the event as one of the Olympic Games' most captivating dramas.

A packed house of seventy-five thousand, including Queen Alexandra, looked on as Pietri entered the Shepherd's Bush stadium ahead of the pack, with under a lap to the finish line. But the gaunt runner was clearly in distress and staggered several times like a man on a bender. Then he fell, and out stepped nattily dressed officials in ties and bowlers to scoop him up and send him in the right direction. Pietri fell four or five more times—and each time, the officials intervened. Their contact was clearly illegal, but the drama went on, with the officials practically throwing the Italian runner across the finish line. Lost in the excitement was the performance of the American, twenty-four-year-old Johnny Hayes of New York City, who chugged into the stadium unaided and unnoticed, finishing just moments later. Pietri was disqualified, giving the gold to Hayes. An assistant to the manager of the sporting goods department at Bloomingdale Brothers in New York, Hayes had trained on a cinder track on the roof of the store. Hayes was America's first Olympic Marathon champion, but Pietri's difficulties captured the world's attention. Moved by his courage, the queen presented the Italian with a silver-gilt cup. In a letter home, an American spectator told his family that he had "just seen the greatest race of the century."

. . .

In Yonkers Weston spoke for forty minutes, shook some hands, and was off again. Pausing briefly up the street at Manor Hall, he was escorted to the Board of Contract Room, where he signed the guestbook. "March 15, 10:35 p.m., Edward Payson Weston, en route New York to San Francisco, 3,400 miles," he wrote, though the projected distance was closer to 3,900 miles. With that, Weston briskly strode back to Broadway to knock off another few brisk miles before bed.

In his twenties and thirties Weston thought nothing of walking late into the night. But with age, he had become more selective—sticking mostly to daylight hours, stopping when he was spent, and resuming only when he was fresh. But there was no need to stop now; invigorated by the attentive crowds, mild weather, and a choice of hotels at which to spend the night, Weston plowed ahead. Continuing northward through the Westchester County river towns of Hastings-on-Hudson, Dobbs Ferry, and Irvington, he would trudge another seven up-and-down miles to Tarrytown, arriving at 1:26 a.m. before bedding down at the Florence, the stately three-story hotel with a wraparound porch and picture-postcard view of the Hudson River. The Florence had a history—according local legend, the cocktail was invented there. No wonder it was a favorite stopping place for a charismatic, young New York City lawyer with a bright future; the twenty-seven-year-old Franklin Delano Roosevelt often spent the night at the Florence en route to his family home in Hyde Park. A year later, Roosevelt would establish himself as a man to watch in politics, winning a seat in the state senate in New York as a Democrat in a Republican district.

So Weston's eventful first day was done. He had covered thirty miles and notched headlines. Weston's walk was a big story on several levels. He was a healthy septuagenarian doing something extraordinary and was a symbol of simpler times in an age of rapid technological change. Perhaps most significant of all, this latest walk was a reminder of just how unique and enduring Weston was as a personality to Americans in 1909. "There is a large significance perhaps in the fact that ever since the beginning of his career as a pedestrian, Edward Payson Weston has kept all three of his names in print," the *Times* would editorialize on March 17. "Nobody would know who was meant by 'E. P. Weston,' and no contraction, affectionate or derisive, has been made to fit him."

The *Times* had it right. "This indicates in its way general recognition of a dignity in the man which is lacking in the vast majority of those famous for proficiency in professional sports and contests—an appreciation of the peculiarity that with him walking has never been an end, but always a means, utilized, more or less sincerely and more or less successfully, for the illustration of certain hygienic theories," the paper wrote. "In other words, Edward Payson Weston has been not so much a pedestrian as a man with a cause, preaching it with a curious and appealing picturesqueness of expression."

Flowery tributes aside, the *Times* had expressed another question in its editorial that was central to this particular walk, the kind that people discussed more in private: could Weston *at the age of seventy* even survive a four-thousand-mile trek? Weston may have been the greatest pedestrian the world had known, but what he attempted was a next-to-impossible task, the equivalent of a marathon a day. It was as if Nolan Ryan or Mariano Rivera, both of them still great well into their forties, were still at it decades later. Of all athletes, perhaps jockeys are the ones most capable of competing into their fifties. "Weston . . . cannot go on making these journeys forever," the newspaper wrote. "Those who know and like the old man best are a good deal worried about the outcome of this one."

2

"I Fancied I Was a Great Actor"

Edward Payson Weston didn't linger at the Florence Hotel in Tarrytown. For years, reporters had marveled about his astounding ability to use a good night's sleep or catnap, a cup of tea, or even a spirited conversation to quickly rebound. Up early for his morning bath on Tuesday, Weston was out the door at 8:00 a.m., resuming his trek northward on Broadway as he waved his hat to a gaggle of shopkeepers.

Past Tarrytown the pavement of Broadway became dirt again, which in mid-March meant a lot of mud. Weston made good time, reaching Ossining, six miles north, in less than two hours, all the time pushing through crowds gathered along the way. The pedestrian was hoping to make it all the way to Poughkeepsie before nightfall, some fifty miles from Tarrytown; but past the sixteen-mile mark at Peekskill, Weston's problems multiplied. Day two of the great transcontinental walk was becoming every bit as eventful as the first.

For starters, there were hills, not steep like the Rockies but more of a series of foothills similar to the Ozarks—up and down, up and down, with little respite. It was difficult. So was a blister that Weston had developed on the ball of his right foot, which he claimed in his newspaper dispatch was the first he had ever had. A man who had walked for nearly fifty years had never sported a single blister? That seemed hard to believe. Then it began snowing, the flakes and biting wind hitting Weston's face as the roads turned icy and hazardous. Adding to the challenge were inaccurate maps, which had underestimated by ten miles the distance to Poughkeepsie, which is actually sixty miles from Tarrytown. But the route's most relentless challenge was the mud—it was everywhere, impossible to avoid, caking Weston's boots and adding weight to each step. Resting in Peekskill for a leisurely two hours and fifteen minutes, in part to ensure his walking companion James Pillow could grab some needed R&R, Weston decided to trudge only another eight miles to Fishkill and no farther.

"I intended to get as far as [another five miles to] Wappinger's Falls . . . but the [road between Peekskill and Fishkill] was simply heart-breaking," he said. "The ground was half frozen and the road nearly impassable for a pedestrian." Despite the mud and the maps, the great pedestrian made the most of things, having chosen his footwear wisely and feeding off the energy from the crowds. "I blessed my stars that I was not such an idiot as to wear any rubber on my shoes as it would have held my feet in the ruts at every step, and I should have strained both ankles before I had gone an hour," Weston said. Past Peekskill, dusk and then darkness set in, and those ruts turned truly perilous, forcing Weston to adopt the slower but time-tested strategy of periodically passing from side to side across the road. "I had to cross and recross the road about fifty times every hour."

Weston's difficulty with the map was a simple screwup by a local map from a jaunt through the area in 1893 that misjudged the distance from Tarrytown to Poughkeepsie. But like many great athletes, Weston didn't linger on the day's disappointment, choosing instead to stay upbeat, revel in the adulation, and look ahead. What wasn't to like? Cordial greetings and best wishes had swamped Weston all day. At many houses, families offered Weston tea, coffee, and eggs and milk; so recognizable his diet had become to anyone who read a newspaper. "The generous hospitality of the people hereabout is unbounded," Weston said, underscoring how far he had traveled from his early, rough-and-tumble days when bettors sometimes tried to run him off the road.

A half century on the road had made Weston a deft touch in public relations. Weston filled his dispatches with praise for people he had met along the way, often describing them as the warmest and most hospitable he had ever met, and he meant it until the next day, by which time he had run into the newest case of astounding graciousness. And often his reviews of a hotel or a meal were so gushing that what innkeeper or restaurant owner wouldn't be eager to have him stay overnight or at least to serve him a slab of homemade pie and coffee? As a people person in a lonely pursuit, Weston courted relationships, particularly with fellow veterans, along with policemen, innkeepers, restaurant owners, and railroad men. He searched his prodigious memory for the names of someone he had met in a small town thirty or forty years before, which never failed to impress the locals on his next trip through that town, when he fondly recalled old Fred or George and won a new cast of admirers.

Weston talked quickly, almost nervously, with his words gushing forth and his hands moving about. Forever quick with a joke or a quip, he connected equally with adults and children. Weston was also exceedingly respectful of local customs and history, having signed the guest book in Yonkers and on day two just north of Peekskill paying a visit to St. Phillip's Cemetery in Garrison at the grave of a fellow veteran, Sergeant Hamilton Fish Jr., a member of Theodore Roosevelt's Park Avenue Contingent in the conflict. Part of a famous Hudson Valley political family, Fish had been the first of the famed Rough Riders to lose his life in the Spanish American War, near Sevilla, Cuba, on June 23, 1898. The locals ate it up.

. . .

Given the considerable challenges on day two of his great transcontinental walk, Weston was anxious for an early start to day three—when he looked for a bit of luck, an omen, anything that could improve the conditions. After all, it was Wednesday, March 17, St. Patrick's Day, a factoid he would duly note in his dispatch to the *New York Times*. And wouldn't you know it, but the weather gods were gazing favorably on the great pedestrian by delivering a day of dry weather that firmed up the dirt road, which eased the stress on Weston's ankles. Even the annoying blister receded. "God is good to the Irish," noted the walkist, with a nod to his heritage. "This was what first impressed me when I first put my foot on the ground in Fishkill," he said. "In an experience of nearly forty-five years I have never enjoyed such a sustaining day or such a grand road as that which I covered between Wappinger's Falls and Rhinebeck. It was superb."

Starting at 6:00 a.m., Weston knocked off those ten miles to Poughkeepsie. Encouraged, he treated himself to breakfast at the Nelson House, the handsome red-brick neocolonial hotel on Market Street once described as "Poughkeepsie's Waldorf-Astoria." Back on the road, Weston steadily wended northward through Franklin Roosevelt's hometown of Hyde Park and at 5:15 p.m. reached Rhinebeck, where a woman pinned a violet on his vest and a two-year-old child presented him with an emerald flag. It was a moment. Weston kissed the child and reveled in the atmosphere. "I am in perfect health, without an ache or a pain and having discouraged blisters the second day out," he gushed. "I shall keep them off with a salt bath each morning."

The Hudson Valley is a visually intoxicating part of America. Speckled with historical homes from the Roosevelt and Vanderbilt residences, stunning river views, and astonishing light and colors, its beauty has inspired generations of artists, including those of the famed Hudson River School. Dotting the landscape are picturesque small towns, prestigious colleges like Vassar and Bard, and even vineyards. But on the evening of March 17, 1909, as darkness descended and the temperature dropped, Edward Payson Weston's perspective of the countryside took a sharp turn for the worse. Halfway along the thirty-two-mile route from Rhinebeck to Hudson, the roads were frozen and riddled with deep grooves and ruts. Every step was treacherous. "Indescribably bad and nearly impassable for man, beast, or automobile . . . the most terrible I have ever encountered," Weston said of the stretch of road.

At least the hamlet of Red Hook, about twenty miles from his day's destination, offered a respite. A mile or so from town, a drum and bugle corps braved the discomfort to greet and noisily escort Weston to a hotel in town, the Stewart House. But having lost time, the old pedestrian lingered only fifteen minutes before pushing on again. A mile or so later, he asked a local how far it was to Hudson.

"Just twenty-two miles," the man said.

Well, that was bad news. "Why, a mile back I was told it was only twenty miles," Weston replied. "Do you think I am a lunatic to be walking the other way?"

"I don't know for sure, boss," the man said. "Haven't known you long enough, but you look it."

Determined to reach Hudson before bedtime, Weston plowed ahead, avoiding some ruts by stepping gingerly, or "figuratively danc[ing] the Salome and 'can can,'" as he put it. Those last four miles took one hour and fifty minutes—but Weston made it, arriving at 1:30 a.m. in Hudson, where Police Chief J. J. Lane was at the city line to greet the weary pedestrian and direct him to lodging. The old pedestrian had covered another sixty miles. An exhausting day three was done, but Weston was back on track and again feeling upbeat.

That would be "on track" but hardly routine. So it went, in the world of long-distance walking, where the weather, the ruts, the aching and sore joints, and all that mud meant the only guarantee was there were no guarantees. It's why some of Weston's daily dispatches were long, detailed, and full of insight, while others, on days when he didn't have the time and inclination or energy, were not. Some days, Weston felt good, which tended to make him chatty. Other times, he was bone tired, too spent to say much, or didn't hold forth because, frankly, the day had been routine. Day four, a thirty-nine-mile trek ever northward to Troy, was one of those times. It's likely that Weston didn't write much about the day because next to his rugged journey of the night before, it wasn't particularly eventful.

But Troy was a landmark in the great trek across America, a place where Weston noted that despite the travails, he had still managed to cover 175 miles in only four days—an average of more than 43 miles a day. An industrial center on the eastern bank of the Hudson River, Troy was at its peak in 1909—a town of seventy-six thousand, many of whom were involved in the city's thriving steel, iron, and shirt- and collar-making industries. Several decades before, Troy had even supported a couple of big-league baseball teams, most recently including the National League's Troy Trojans, which a quarter century before had left for New York City and become the Giants. It was here that Weston planned to turn sharply west over the Hudson River and traverse New York's Mohawk River Valley—through Utica and Syracuse toward Rochester, roughly parallel to the route of today's New York Thruway.

Troy's enthusiastic reception thrilled and revived Weston. Arriving just after midnight, he was met by a fired-up crowd of fifteen hundred people. It was the early twentieth-century version of the flash mob, ably assembled with the help of newspaper accounts, telephone calls, and word of mouth. Spending the night at the Rensselaer Hotel, Weston slept well and enjoyed a hearty breakfast. Then at 7:00 a.m. he pushed off along a trolley road toward Schenectady and was encouraged by the greetings from residents en route. "Women, children, workmen, and boys were lined up waiting for me to pass," Weston gushed. "[I] was amazed at the enthusiastic greetings."

Seven miles west of Troy—about halfway to Schenectady—Weston tripped and tumbled to the trolley tracks. Walking across America could be hazardous; Weston had fallen hard, winding up on his back, staring skyward, and "studying astronomy," as he would put it. But as quickly as he had fallen, Weston was back on his feet in a jiffy and on his way. An hour or so later, the episode had become another footnote as Weston entered Schenectady to a sea of thousands of well-wishers. Some had arrived in cars and carriages; others lined the sidewalks as Weston headed down State Street to the Edison Hotel, where he would enjoy a brief rest. "The applause was so loud and enthusiastic that I fancied I was a great actor."

In a sense, he was. Weston basked in Schenectady's warm embrace, bowing this way and that way as if he were on Broadway. It's part of what branded him as the master of his sport and would put him on a sports card in 1910 as part of Mecca Cigarettes' t218 set of 153 "Champion Athletes." The cards measure two and a half inches by two and seven-eighths inches and feature a cast of athletes from prizefighting to track and field, golf, and even billiards. Weston appears in a handsome color drawing on the front, with Mecca advertising and a short biography on back. "Edward Payson Weston is probably the greatest pedestrian that ever lived," reads the card.

The Weston card isn't valuable—Dave's Vintage Baseball Cards of Los Angeles offered one recently in "very good-to-excellent" condition for $15.20. That's a big contrast to baseball cards from the era, some of which fetch prices in the thousands or millions in the case of the famed Honus Wagner t206 card. But the Weston card fit right into the early twentieth-century mania of card collecting—and more than a century later helps to keep his name before card collectors.

After resting two hours at the Edison Hotel, Weston was on

the road again in hopes of knocking off another thirty-one miles to Fonda. Eight miles later, the pedestrian toppled over again, catching his foot in a wire loop attached to a heavy weight and landing in a sea of mud. In the accident, Weston pinned his left arm, which would ache for days. Taking stock, Weston counted his blessings—"grateful," he said, "that neither feet nor legs were injured," and so much so "that I can easily endure the pain in the arm." As a result, Weston didn't stop again the rest of the day—heading just before 6:00 p.m. through Amsterdam, festooned in flags in his honor. Three hours later, he was in Fonda, heartily welcomed by the mayor and police chief, and relieved to be there. Forty-five more miles—and a total of 220 in five days—were in the books.

More calamities were just ahead. Cracking open the door of his Fonda hotel at 5:10 a.m. on Saturday, March 20, Weston stared at a winter wonderland: a fresh coat of four inches of snow and swirling winds of forty-five miles per hour. But stop? Out of the question. Fifty minutes later, a tire blew out on Weston's car, sending his driver back to town in search of a garage and leaving the pedestrian to plow on alone, enduring grooves in the road and snow drifts that reached ten feet. Weston's goal for the day was to cover the fifty-five miles to Utica and the prom- ise of a blessed Sunday of rest. "Slow walking and hard work," he said of his ordeal, which after four hours found him near the hamlet of Palatine Bridge, nine miles east of St. Johnsville, and feeling hungry and faint. This was "no easy task even for the toughest man."

Years on the road had taught Weston when to admit he was licked and needed help. It was one of those times. And where exactly was his car? Alone, cold, and in desperate need of a pick-me-up, Weston was passing the cozy and well-appointed home of one J. S. Ellithorp, who called out a hearty "good morning" and invited him into his living room. "If ever a ship- wrecked mariner found joy in reaching a haven of safety, I was more than glad," Weston said. Seldom had a steaming cup of coffee, a couple of eggs, and dry toast done more good. Revived, Weston was back on the road by midday bound for St. Johnsville.

This time, it was a uniformed twenty-one-piece traveling show that met Weston just outside town and escorted him to the Kyser House Hotel. The weekend shopping crowd lined the streets of St. Johnsville and cheered—presumably for Weston, not the traveling show. Stopping briefly, Weston was soon back on the road, trekking steadily westward through a progression of postage-stamp-sized towns like Little Falls, Mohawk, Ilion, and Frankfort. Determined to reach Utica, Weston stopped only once that afternoon, a ten-minute respite for a bowl of soup in Herkimer. Like a commuter anxious to get home after a long day, he moved briskly, reaching town at midnight. The snowy day had been hard, but remarkably Weston had covered 60 miles to reach his first week's goal of 275 miles into his walk across America. The weather had slowed but not beaten the old pedestrian. But with winter's grasp still blanketing upstate New York, difficult days were ahead.

3

"Pride and Pluck Had Prevailed"

Utica was wild for Edward Payson Weston. More than two thousand people, some undoubtedly thinking this could be Weston's last great walk, crammed the downtown streets at midnight to see him arrive. Grateful for the attention, the old pedestrian was exhausted and looking forward to a welcome day of R & R. That he was staying at the Baggs Hotel had put an extra bounce in his step in the final hours of Saturday's walk. On previous visits, Weston had enjoyed both the hospitality and something else there: "the best coffee . . . that I ever found in any hotel."

Rest brought reflection to what had been an eventful first week. First came an apology. "An honest confession is good for the soul," Weston said, "and in giving a story generalizing the walk from New York this far, I want . . . to apologize to those friends, who were in the Post Office in New York to bid me Godspeed, for leaving them so abruptly and hastening to the street." Next came the pedestrian's confession that he had suffered a severe injury to his left foot eleven weeks prior, which had caused "great pain and frightened [him] to death" that he would need to postpone the great walk westward. That hadn't happened, but on the advice of his physicians, Weston had sharply curtailed his training to no more than five miles a day in the seven weeks before the walk. It was hardly the kind of extensive preparation needed for a seventy-year-old man about to traverse the continent.

The caution paid off. Assured by his doctors that he was fit enough to leave on schedule, Weston had launched his great walk the previous Monday while still feeling unsteady and decidedly unconfident. But basking in the instant and often overwhelming adulation of the crowds who lined the streets of Manhattan to see him off had done a world of good, more to cure his ailing foot than any kind of wrap, bandage, or medical treatment ever could. "When I saw the great enthusiastic throng and the genial friends who greeted me all through the walk to 125th Street . . . I was praying every step I took that no one would ever have the chance to say to them, 'I told you so.'" For Weston, it was the first sign that the walk was meant to happen. Sign number two came that Monday evening as he arrived in Tarrytown, having marched thirty miles and felt no apparent discomfort. "I lay no pretentions to piety," Weston said, "but common sense teaches all of us that there is a God in everything, and my experience of the last five days . . . has assured me that he is with me in this effort."

Weston took his successful treatment of that annoying blister as another sign that he was destined to complete his walk to the West Coast. Anyone who has ever walked, hiked, or run ought to recognize the pain of an untreated blister. How fortunate that Weston was able to effectively treat it by popping the inflammation with a needle, followed by a salt water bath and drying and applying lotion to the afflicted area. To be sure, he repeated his home remedy that afternoon sixteen miles up the road in Peekskill during a rest stop—"settl[ing] the blister situation for the entire route."

Then Weston discovered another sign that he had made the right choice in deciding to begin walking in New York. One week into his trek, the pedestrian had passed the ultimate test, persevering through some of the worst road conditions and most punishing cold he had encountered. At age seventy, he still had what it takes, particularly on the road north of Poughkeepsie—"one long continuation of frozen, narrow, deep mud ruts where one had to keep his footing with care," as Weston called it. During those final four miles into Hudson, the old pedestrian's pride had kicked in and practically willed him forward. "Had it not been for constantly thinking that if I failed to get to Hudson that night, my [friends] would think I was growing weak," Weston said. "It would then be a question whether pride, principle, or pluck would get the best of it." Pluck had prevailed. "For the first time in my public career," he said in Utica, "I am amazed at myself and what I have accomplished during the last week."

. . .

Zigzagging to avoid the ruts on the road north of Peekskill. Stopping periodically for coffee and a chat along the way. Knowing when to replenish himself, how long to stop, and the right footwear to wear. For all the hardships that Edward Payson Weston endured in that first week of walking from New York City to Utica, there wasn't much he hadn't faced already in nearly fifty years of roaming. Though Weston had been perfecting his routines for the road for years, it's remarkable how many successful techniques the great pedestrian had established back in the winter of 1861 in his first great walk—which he then stuck with for the long haul. Just as remarkable is how he used that first great walk to single-handedly launch America's pedestrianism craze.

Weston didn't invent walking. He just walked farther, at a faster pace, and for more years than anyone else, making his able ambulation both profitable and a wonder of the age. It's hard to put precise dates on when exactly distance walking had become popular. It may have been somewhere between 8000 and 10,000 BC—or BB for "Before Birkenstocks" according to

About.com—when Native Americans started what may have been one of the first fashion trends by styling easy-to-wear sandals with sling backs. In AD 100 Emperor Hadrian, presumably wearing something sturdier than slip-ons, marched twenty-one miles a day in full armor, touring his empire entirely on foot. As the centuries passed, distance walking grew steadily more popular, particularly among Great Britain's landed gentry. In 1589 Sir Robert Casey, on a bet, ambled three hundred miles from London to Berwick. In the 1600s King Charles II racewalked from Whitehall in central London to Hampton Court, a distance of about twelve miles. Then, in 1762, John Hague set out to walk one hundred miles in twenty-four hours, meeting his goal with forty-five minutes to spare.

No one can pinpoint where and when professional walking began. Most likely it was during the late eighteenth century in Britain and involved a lot of wagering. By then, there was no shortage of long-distance pedestrians, ranging from a Lieutenant Halifax, who one-upped John Hague by walking six hundred miles in twenty days and two hundred miles in one hundred hours, to another calling himself "Child, the Miller of Wandsworth," who set out to walk forty-five miles in eight hours and made it with three minutes left—presumably to profitable ends. In 1790 Foster Powell bet he could walk from London to York and back again—about 350 miles—in five days and eighteen hours. He made it with two hours remaining, winning the bet of "20 guineas to 13." A Mr. Downs made it as well, ambling four hundred miles in ten days in 1808 and then thirty-five miles a day for twenty straight days.

But no one in early nineteenth-century Britain profited more from walking than Captain Robert Barclay Allardice. One of early pedestrianism's great characters, Allardice was an aristocratic Scot whose sizable family income afforded him the luxury of pursuing the pleasures of the "fancy," the name for the wealthy and often dissolute members of the aristocracy interested mostly in horse racing and prizefighting. The captain became the best-known pedestrian of the era, a forefather of the British tradition that cherished walking for competition and exercise. Two of the leading Romantic poets, Wordsworth and Coleridge, were avid walkers and often rambled twenty to thirty miles a day while composing poems. Charles Dickens was a walkist too, every evening averaging a trek of a dozen miles, without which, he said, "I should just explode and perish."

Allardice himself often walked up to seventy miles a day for pleasure. Finding he could parlay an uncanny ability to walk extraordinary distances into winning large amounts of money, the captain in 1809 covered one thousand miles in one thousand hours, clearing an even one thousand guineas. At first, that doesn't sound especially difficult, but it meant he had to endure six weeks of sleep deprivation. "Even walking 1,000 miles in just less than six weeks is well within the range of the possible," writes Geoff Nicholson in his 2008 book, *The Lost Art of Walking.* "The problem is having to walk just a mile in every single hour. Think about it." The captain's feat was a sensation, attracting vast crowds and the wagering of more than £100,000, the equivalent of £4 million in today's currency. That the captain made it and earned a fortune must have pleased him. That he made it and got to take a good long nap must have pleased him more. In later years, he became a trainer of athletes, when the very concept of preparing for a sporting event was something new. In his seventies, Allardice could still lift a fully grown man standing on his open hand from the floor and place him upright on top of a table.

By the mid-nineteenth century, Americans had caught on to the joys of walking, though not as avidly as the British, who had more of a leisure class to make it happen. Pedestrianism's biggest U.S. advocates were writers like Washington Irving and Mark Twain, whose characters were often roamers. Irving's best-known character, Rip Van Winkle, was an indifferent walker, given to wandering the small towns of New York's Catskill Mountains when he wasn't slacking off or indulging in a twenty-year snooze. Irving would celebrate his own wanderings throughout Spain in his 1832 book, *The Alhambra: A Series of Tales and Sketches of the Moors and Spaniards*.

Twain's works were chockablock full of wanderers turned walkists. Huckleberry Finn and his partner in mischief, Tom Sawyer, walked here, there, and everywhere in their adventures. So did the grandly named Butterworth Stavely, an American adventurer who instigates a coup d'état and has himself crowned Butterworth I, Emperor of Pitcairn's Island in Twain's 1879 farce, *The Great Revolution in Pitcairn*. Less known but just as hilarious were the two raffish grifters from *The Adventures of Huckleberry Finn*, the King and the Duke, who walked when they could but who also had to run from one angry mob or another. Claiming to be the son of an English duke (the Duke of Bridgewater) and the lost dauphin, the son of Louis XVI, the two delightful rogues join Huck and Jim on their raft, committing confidence schemes on the way south and snookering the locals until they're run off—on foot, of course, and just ahead of the pursuing posse.

When Henry David Thoreau wasn't contemplating life at Walden Pond, he walked. "I think that I cannot preserve my health and spirits," he wrote in a celebrated essay, *Walking*, "unless I spend four hours a day at least—and it is commonly more than that—sauntering through the woods and over the hills and fields, absolutely free from all worldly engagements."

"I, who cannot stay in my chamber for a single day without acquiring some rust, and when sometimes I have stolen forth for a walk at the 11th hour, or at 4 o'clock in the afternoon, too late to redeem the day, when the shades of night were already beginning to be mingled with the daylight, have felt as if I had committed some sin to be atoned for," Thoreau wrote. "I confess that I am astounded at the power of endurance, to say nothing of my neighbors who confine themselves to shops and offices the whole day for weeks and months, aye, and years almost together. I know not what manner of stuff they are—sitting there now at 3 o'clock in the afternoon, as if it were 3 o'clock in the morning." Thoreau wrote and rewrote his essay throughout the 1850s, though it only appeared in print in the *Atlantic Monthly* of June 1862, the month after his death. The essay is considered a doctrine of the U.S. environmental movement.

About the time Thoreau was waxing poetic about the joys of walking, a whole generation of dreamers, schemers, and American originals had established a tradition of rambling as wide as the American continent. The late eighteenth-century pioneer Johnny Appleseed, born John Chapman, was a walker for most of his seventy years, becoming a celebrated American nurseryman, missionary, and mystic best known for introducing apple trees to large tracts of Ohio, Indiana, and Illinois. A century or so later, in 1865, New York newspaper editor Horace Greeley wrote, "Go West, young man," in what became a mantra—and millions did just that, via railroads, ocean voyage, stagecoaches, horses, and on foot. In hindsight Greeley's advice was a tad ironic; for in 1859 he took his own advice, crossing the country in a stagecoach and hating much of what he saw. Native Americans, he wrote, "are children," and "their arts, wars, treaties, alliances, habitations, crafts, properties, commerce, comforts, all belong to the very lowest and rudest ages of human existence." Nor did Greely think much of the country, with the Great Plains earning his particular wrath. "Nearly destitute of human inhabitants," the plains were "treeless, cheerless, forbidding," he wrote. He even had sour words for the Humboldt River of northern Nevada—a river for goodness' sake!—calling it "the meanest . . . of its length on earth." No wonder Greeley was happier suggesting that others head west.

For the big westward ramble, the Lewis and Clark expedition of 1804 to 1806 set a precedent. For the first-ever U.S.

expedition to the Pacific Coast, President Thomas Jefferson commissioned two Virginia-born veterans of Indian wars in the Ohio Valley, Meriwether Lewis and William Clark, to chart the area's plants, animal life, and geography, in order to discover how the region could be exploited economically. Proceeding largely on horseback, the party were often forced to walk, particularly through the Rockies. Before long, untold millions were heading west, turning former Indian trails into roads and highways—hitting the road in search of work, the promise of land, opportunity, and a fresh start in wide-open spaces beyond the ever-increasing density of the East Coast.

Many of the settlers throughout the wide-open spaces of the United States were immigrants who left Europe to become laborers, miners, and steel workers, or as mail-order brides. Filling the wheat fields and small towns of the inner continent with the sounds of Italian, Hungarian, Yiddish, and Norwegian, they helped transform America into a vast, mobile society dependent on transportation and often a strong set of legs. Those on the move included a whole generation of eccentrics, drifters, and artists, for whom walking was part of their lives. And among the walkers of that time were many who chose to stick closer to home: the more than 69 percent of the U.S. labor force in 1840 who were farmers. Though the percentage of farmers would drop consistently—from 58 percent of the 1860 labor force to 31 percent in 1910—their numbers were still significant. Suffice it to say that a much bigger percentage of the population in those days led a strenuous, active life—covering more miles on foot in a week than most of us nowadays do in a year.

In 1883 a man wearing a sixty-pound suit, sewn with leather boot tops from head to toe, and known as the Old Leatherman started to continuously walk a 365-mile loop between Connecticut and the Hudson River valley towns of New York. It would take the Old Leatherman precisely thirty-four days to complete the circuit, which he did mostly on schedule, give or take a day here and there, for the next six years, sleeping along the way in caves and a series of crude homemade storm shelters. So punctual were the Leatherman's habits that the people who slipped him handouts and spare change could practically set their watches by him. One store even kept a copy of his order: "One loaf of bread, a can of sardines, one pound of fancy crackers, a pie, two quarts of coffee, one gill of brandy, and a bottle of beer."

It was news when the Old Leatherman hit town—or didn't because he had fallen behind in his travels. He became a regular news story, as a familiar presence and a mystery man who rarely if ever was heard to utter an intelligible word. Asked by reporters about his background or philosophy, the wandering soul would slink away saying nothing. That only intensified the interest and mystique about the Leatherman, so much so that ten Connecticut towns passed ordinances exempting him from the state's antitramp law.

Stories and rumors about the Old Leatherman's true identity were rampant. Some thought he was Catholic because he declined Friday handouts of meat. Others believed he was a Frenchman named Jules Bourglay, a native of Lyons who knew next to no English. According to legend, Bourglay had been a wood-carver in France, when he fell in love with the daughter of a wealthy merchant. Asking for the girl's hand in marriage, Bourglay wasn't told yes or no but was given a job in her father's leather business for one year in order to prove himself so he could marry her. But between a depressed market and Bourglay's questionable business acumen, the internship was a failure, and the young man was let go. The wedding was off, as the story goes, sending a distraught Bourglay to a French monastery and then to America, where he began walking compulsively to ease his grief. It's a colorful tale, but a more likely explanation is that the Old Leatherman walked compulsively and didn't communicate because of mental illness.

In 1889 the Leatherman passed away from cancer of the mouth caused by tobacco use. Though the Connecticut Humane Society had planned to treat him for his illness, the old wanderer was found dead in his Saw Mill Woods cave near Ossining, New York, right off Broadway and a stone's throw from where Weston would pass in 1909. Buried at Sparta Cemetery in Scarborough, New York, the Leatherman's body was exhumed in early 2011 and reburied in a new pine coffin.

By the late nineteenth century women were walking as well, some to great acclaim. In 1896 a Norwegian immigrant and mother of eight named Helga Estby left her home in eastern Washington State and trekked all the way to New York, drawn by the promise of a $10,000 prize. Accompanied by her teenage daughter, Clara, and armed with little beyond a compass, a curling iron, and a revolver, Estby wended through fourteen states and enough adventure to fill a book. Helga Estby would endure withering criticism of her trek from those who thought a woman's place was at home with no questions asked, and she never earned a dime for her effort. No wonder she seldom spoke of her trip and it took more than a century for a book to be written about her remarkable accomplishment.

. . .

Weston was neither a tramp nor a fancy. On the eve of his first great walk in 1861, he was a middle-class twenty-one-year-old clerk bearing a striking resemblance to Jimmy Cagney and a healthy touch of wanderlust. Born March 15, 1839, in Providence, Rhode Island, to Silas and Marie Gaines Weston, Edward checked in on the small side—at four pounds, six ounces—and from all accounts was a bright, lively child with a hint of the restlessness to come. Weston's great-granddaughter, Joyce Litz, wrote that Edward at birth was so frail that he wasn't expected to live. Described as "weak and sickly" as a youngster, Weston was remembered years later by his minister, Reverend J. C. Fletcher, as lean, engaging, and easily able to ace his Sunday school lessons. "But," said the good reverend, "Edward Payson Weston was the most uneasy bright boy I ever saw. There was no keeping him still." Most likely, he was hyperactive.

Known as Eddy, Weston was the second of four children and the family's only son. He was ten years old when his merchant father left his family for the gold rush in California; and though it's anyone's guess what affect the trip had on the young boy, it may have triggered a lifelong romance of the rambling life. That winter, a famous group of traveling singers, the Hutchinson Family, visited the area, and young Weston pleaded with his mother to grant him permission to leave home and tour with the group. The Hutchinsons were a big extended family—various combinations of the thirteen children of Jesse Hutchinson, a farmer from Milford, New Hampshire, and his wife Mary, who often sang about rural life and social issues from abolition and temperance to politics and women's suffrage. The Hutchinson Family Singers not only established an impressive musical legacy, but they also are considered among the forerunners of the great protest singers and folk groups of the twentieth century.

Pestering his mother for permission to leave home and join the singing troupe was an introduction of sorts to Weston's iron will. He pleaded and pleaded some more, until Mrs. Weston finally let the ten-year-old set off with the Hutchinsons for a year-long traipsing about America to sell candy and songbooks during concerts. Back home at age eleven, Weston soon took off again, this time for Lynn, Massachusetts, to live with Jesse and Mary Hutchinson and several of their children.

Permitting a sickly ten-year-old child to leave home is unusual parenting for any era. But Silas and Marie Gaines Weston were a different kind of couple. It started with their appearance: At six feet four inches, Silas towered over most everyone he met at a time when the average height for men was only five feet seven and a half inches. A New Hampshire native, he wrote poetry and played the bass viol or viola da gamba, an instrument usually associated with the Renaissance and Baroque periods. The Westons weren't poor; and according to the 1850 census, they appeared to have a live-in housekeeper. But from all accounts, Silas, incapable of making a steady living and careless with money, was troubled in business. Though he was often away in search of the next "big thing," he never displayed any ability for business.

On the other hand, Marie has been described by Joyce Litz as delicate looking, although the Massachusetts native was a formidable person—a romance novelist of some repute and, in the decade before the Civil War, a part of New England's literary abolitionist set. Using the pen name M. D. Gaines, in 1859, Marie wrote her best-known novel, *Kate Felton; or, A Peep at Realities*, which took a strong stand against slavery. Chances are, her role model was a fellow member of the Boston abolitionist crowd: Harriet Beecher Stowe, author of *Uncle Tom's Cabin*, published in 1851. Marie Weston's other novel, published in 1866, was *Bessie and Raymond; or, Incidents Connected with the Civil War in the United States.*

In the meantime, young Eddie Weston's love for the road evolved, fortified by restlessness, a gift for gab, and a flourishing entrepreneurial flair. Rejoining his family after they moved to Boston, he balanced school and a position selling candy at the old Ordway Hall theater. By then, his father was back from California, apparently no wealthier for the experience but filled with colorful tales of life in the West. Captivated, the youngster in 1853 took a page from his mother's literary career and published a pamphlet describing his father's adventures. That Weston drew so much inspiration from his mother isn't surprising. He and Marie would clash over his decision to become a professional walkist, but Weston's vow never to walk on Sunday was the result of that close relationship and the promise he had made to her. Years later, Weston related another experience, which happened on the last leg of a scorching hot walk when facing a three-mile climb up a hill. He began lurching and struggling in exhaustion, only to see a vision of his mother praying that he find the strength to reach the top. Fortified by his vision, Weston felt revived and made it to the top.

In his teens, Eddie Weston's health remained precarious. So frail that he was often in bed, the teenager caught the eye of a family friend, a sports trainer, who convinced the family he could help the boy. He took Edward off coffee and put him on a strict regimen of vegetables and milk. When the trainer suggested he take a short walk every day for exercise, Weston took him up and found both the freedom and the fresh air invigorating. The regimen helped, and by 1855 Edward's health was so much improved that it gave the teenager the confidence to take off again—this time selling candy and newspapers along with quite a few copies of his father's pamphlet on the Boston, Providence, and Stonington Railroad. A year later, Weston found a similar position aboard the *Empire State*, a steamship sailing between Fall River, Massachusetts, and New York. But at the urging of his father, he moved home to Boston, where Silas secured young Weston with a more sedentary job as a clerk in a merchant's office.

Office work didn't suit Edward Payson Weston. Forever restless, he took another position secured by his father as a jeweler's apprentice but disliked that job as well. So off went Weston again, in the spring of 1856, about the time of his seventeenth birthday, this time joining a traveling circus. Working under an assumed name—most likely to escape detection back home—Weston stuck with it until the following June, when traveling on a wagon outside Lowell, Massachusetts, a bolt of lightning nearly killed him. Traumatized, he refused to enter the circus ring and was fired. Drifting to Canada, he found a job as a drummer for another circus, this one at Spalding and Rogers Circus in Quebec. There was a catch: Weston had never played the drums, but he was fortunate to be mentored by a bugler named Edward Kendall and his son, George, who grew close to the youngster, treating him like a family member.

The Kendalls were a salvation for young Weston. He was able to overcome his fear of lightning and soon regained a sense of steadiness and self-confidence. And this time, Weston stuck to it, touring with the circus throughout Canada and the western United States until the winter of 1856, when it disbanded in Cincinnati. Hopping aboard a train bound for New York, Weston decided on yet another career change. Looking to match his earlier success in hawking pamphlets and newspapers, he decided to walk door-to-door selling books, including ones written by his mother.

. . .

Weston was nineteen and working as a copyboy at the *New York Herald* during an ordinary winter day in February 1859, when his future flashed before him. Put in charge of handling a box of hothouse flowers—the gift from the editor's wife to the U.S. postmaster—Weston was given a simple task. He was to take the flowers from a delivery wagon sent from the editor's home to the newspaper building in Herald Square and hold them for a delivery a block west at Pennsylvania Station for the 6:00 p.m. train to Washington DC.

But Weston plum forgot that it had been his job to unload the box. At 3:00 p.m., when the deliveryman called the office to collect the box headed for the train station, the wagon with the flowers had already left the newspaper office for points farther uptown. Panicked, Weston did the only thing he could have—taking off at a furious clip through the congested streets of Manhattan to find the wagon and retrieve the box. His colleagues scoffed. Make it? Not in a million years, they jeered. Why not just quit now—he was sure to be fired anyway.

But Weston was banking on several advantages. He knew the wagon was headed north, which more than likely meant it was somewhere along Broadway, Manhattan's main thoroughfare. He was right. Also, he figured the midafternoon traffic would be snarled as it usually was most weekdays, holding up the wagon and giving him time to catch up. Right again. And the wiry Weston knew he had the speed and agility to quickly cover ground.

So hightailing it from West Thirty-Forth Street up Broadway, Weston scanned the street for the wagon, catching up to it nearly two miles north at West Seventieth Street. Retrieving the flowers, Weston hopped on a streetcar for the return trip to the *Herald*. Back at work just after 5:00 p.m., Weston made sure the box of flowers was on the way to Washington DC on the 6:00 p.m. train after all. Weston's coworkers were impressed. So was the editor, who, on hearing of his young messenger's determination, doubled his salary to six dollars a week. It got Weston thinking that his uncanny ability to walk quickly for long distances without tiring set him apart. The question was how to exploit that skill.

Around then Weston's father died, and the New York copyboy returned to Massachusetts to support his mother. Resorting to his old standby job of selling books door-to-door afforded Weston the ability to blend a love of rambling long distances with his acumen as a salesman. In 1860 Weston was living in Hartford when he and one George B. Eddy of Worcester, Massachusetts, made their fateful bet: depending on who won that fall's presidential election, the loser of the bet would walk all 478 miles from the steps of the State House in Boston to the U.S. Capitol in Washington DC. And they would have to arrive in ten days for the start of the presidential inauguration on March 4, 1861.

Weston would do the walking if Abraham Lincoln's opponent, George McClellan, lost the election. Eddy would go
if Lincoln lost. Neither man made the wager thinking he
would actually be stuck making the trip. "It was simply banter between ourselves while dining together one day, and I do
not suppose that either of us at that time had the remotest idea
of ever attempting such a task," Weston said. "I was not aware,
at the time, that I possessed any great locomotive powers."
Eddy felt the same, frequently telling Weston that should he
be the victim, he should "most decidedly have preferred not
to be excused."

Every schoolchild knows what happened next. Lincoln won
a splintered race. The election meant Weston would do the
walking—and needed to start contemplating the logistics of such
a journey. How many miles a day would be doable? Where and
how would he eat and sleep? What would he wear to protect
himself from winter? Could he even afford it? Getting busy,
Weston on Christmas Day rented a carriage to carry supplies
for eighty dollars and asked a friend, Charles Foster, to be its
driver and follow the pedestrian at a discreet distance. Maybe
it was the holiday eggnog, but Foster and another friend, Abner
Smith, agreed to drive and distribute brochures from a couple of sponsors that Weston had secured. One of the booklets
described wonders of the Grover and Baker sewing machines
and featured Weston's photo. The other, from the Rubber Clothing Company, would prove more important for Weston; as part
of the agreement, the company gave him one of its rubber suits
that would come in handy in the winter wet and snow.

Looking to work himself into tip-top distance-walking condition, Weston celebrated New Year's Day in 1861 by trekking
thirty-six miles from Hartford to New Haven in ten hours and
forty minutes, dropping off circulars for books en route. The
next day, he returned to Hartford in eleven hours and thirty
minutes, while stopping again at most of the houses he had can-

vassed the day before, in order to sell some books. Anxious to test his endurance, Weston walked January 25 from New Haven to Hartford and back again—tacking on four miles to sell books in Wallingford and covering seventy-six miles total in less than twenty-four hours. Curious to see how he would feel the next morning, he arose and, feeling no worse for wear, went to church. The only victim of all those miles were his shoes, shredded from the rough conditions of the roads. The walkist was nearing his departure more than ready for the big trek.

On February 22 Weston arrived at the State House in Boston, ready with a quip and looking for a swift start. Judging by the few preceding days, when Weston had been hounded by several creditors demanding to be paid, walking was easier than sticking around home. From the steps of the State House, Weston used his bully pulpit to blame them for crassly seizing the most noticeable opportunity to demand payment. It was his first great populist moment, and it riled up the crowd, many of whom shouted, "Shame on them!" Weston hadn't wagered any cash on his walk, he reminded them, but he had bet several bags of peanuts that he would make it on time to Washington DC. So, accompanied by loud cheers, Edward Payson Weston was on his way south—and into legend.

4

"Undeterred, Undismayed, No Matter What Confronts Him"

And on Sunday, he rested—that is, Edward Payson Weston spent his time recuperating and prepping for Monday's sizable fifty-six-mile jaunt from Utica to Syracuse. Though Weston had woken at 11:00 a.m. Sunday, too revved up to get back to sleep, the leisure time restored him. He couldn't wait to get back on the road early Monday; not only did he feel better, but it had stopped snowing. Why not take advantage of the first break in the weather in days?

So there was Weston stepping from the door to the Baggs Hotel in Utica at 11:40 p.m. Sunday, intent on retracing his steps to the eastern outskirts of town to begin his walk. Setting off at 12:05 a.m. for Syracuse, he made good time on the first three miles to Oneida Castle thanks to the state road packed hard with dirt. This was turning into a promising day indeed.

However, prospects quickly dimmed in Oneida, because that same state road soon turned to mud, remaining that way to the city limits of Syracuse, especially for the last thirty miles or so from Chittenango. Spared of another snowstorm, it still amounted to a tedious day of slogging for Weston, who called the last half of his journey, "the most hazardous I ever encountered in my many years of pedestrianism." That would be the *most* hazardous since last week. Though Weston often spoke in such superlatives, his many admirers were willing to overlook the occasional editorial embellishment: after the day's journey, the old athlete was exhausted enough that it probably was the most hazardous, until the next "most" hazardous later in the week. "I thought the frozen roads were the limit, but they weren't," Weston said. "The route through the red clay swamp, which required ten straight hours of plodding, broke the record for bad roads." Each step, Weston said, meant sinking his foot into ankle-deep mud and bringing up at least five pounds of the gooey mess. Slowed to three miles per hour from his usual four, Weston soon felt the strain that started in his ankles and shot to his knees. "At times, it almost seemed that I must give up, but then I brought my Three Musketeers—pride, principle, and pluck—into action, and [I became] a fighting man once more," he added, referring to the name he had given his trio of backers. "I fought the battle and won."

An eventful second week was underway. There was the walking, and then there was everything else, beginning with Weston's lecture that Monday evening in Syracuse, which rendered him so utterly exhausted "that I scarcely remember what I did." There was all the mud to deal with on the roads, which he also had to clean from his boots each evening. And there was the probability of more snow. At least he would be headed south by week's end, toward Pennsylvania and perhaps more temperate temperatures. After spending the first five hundred miles in New York, getting to Pennsylvania, state number two, would mark a milestone of sorts; though Weston was headed all the way to California, he would be passing through only twelve states.

Weston had a timetable but often fell behind, forcing him to improvise. Weather frequently slowed him down, as did nagging injuries. And there were other factors, such as on Tuesday, March 23, between Syracuse and tiny Lyons, when Weston, a social man in a lonely sport, fell into a familiar pattern and got distracted. Leaving Syracuse at 6:00 a.m., he walked a mile before stopping for an hour at the home of an old friend, George Ryan. Feeling relaxed and in a visiting mood, Weston convinced the Ryans and Syracuse policeman F. R. Cander, who had accompanied him from town, to hop in their car and follow him for the next hour so they could keep chatting. Up the road, Weston stopped to see another acquaintance, a former classmate, George Washington Corey, before starting in earnest on the day's task. It had been a welcome break of a few hours and a sign that a good day was ahead in the welcome form of a state road in good condition—"the best stretch of nineteen miles I have seen"—underscored by several rousing receptions in towns along the way.

In Camillus, just west of Syracuse, Weston's arrival prompted the local version of July 4 and New Year's Eve rolled into one. Schools closed for the morning as two hundred students headed two miles east of town to accompany Weston into the town center, while factory whistles shrieked a hearty welcome. Two miles beyond Camillus, Weston reveled in a more intimate gathering: the Hill family's welcome offering of two eggs chased down by several glasses of milk. It more than fortified the old pedestrian for the twelve-mile leg into Weedsport, where school children met and escorted him to the Willard Hotel. The encounters, big and small, meant as much to Weston as a helping of milk with eggs—picking up the old pedestrian after a hard stretch and showering him with welcome attention after long stretches of solitary walking.

No wonder Weston lingered in Weedsport for more than three hours before resuming his journey to Lyons at 5:45 p.m. It had been a more social day than usual—and why not? The walkist deserved days like this one. But east of Lyons, the roads deteriorated, slowing his pace considerably and worrying Weston that he would turn an ankle in the ruts. By 2:30 a.m., six miles from Lyons, he threw in the towel. Pounding on the door of a farmer named C. A. Smith, Weston and his party asked to stay there the rest of the night. Of course they could, which they did for the next four and a half hours. Back on the road by 7:00 a.m., the party reached Lyons two hours later and kept walking. Later in the morning, Weston was in Newark, lunching at the Gardner Hotel. And thirty-two miles after that, thanks to some good roads and several police escorts, he was in Rochester, having trudged forty-nine miles that day in a route that paralleled much of the Erie Canal. One YMCA lecture later, he was asleep by 11:00 p.m. and feeling good.

. . .

There was a reason Weston was so upbeat. In nine days of walking, he had covered 429 miles, an average of nearly of 46 miles a day, many of them accomplished in harsh conditions. Since the hard day's journey into Troy, he had made considerable progress, averaging just short of 52 miles a day, though in all that mud, it must have felt like 90. And despite all those ruts, his ankles felt strong.

But peering into the darkness from his window at the Rochester Hotel at 5:00 a.m. on Thursday, March 25, Weston saw a bleak scene. The snow had fallen all night and showed little sign of letting up. Weston delayed his start by three hours, but the storm kept raging. At 8:00 a.m. Weston figured the worst was over and took off. It was a big mistake. The snow became a blizzard fueled by winds of forty miles per hour. Ducking into the home of C. C. Palmer on Seneca Street, Weston donned his oilskin suit and accepted the gift of a handkerchief, which he wrapped around his neck. It was another example of the random kindness of strangers whom Weston attracted day after day. Mr. Palmer not only gave him the handkerchief but adjusted it, the walkist said, so "that I should not get pneumonia."

The handkerchief worked to a point. Weston avoided pneumonia and steadily forged through the teeth of the gale for eleven miles or so into Churchville, all in hopes of reaching Corfu, another twenty-nine miles away. But leaving town at about 4:15 p.m., the old pedestrian found the snow more than a foot deep and the winds blowing fifty miles per hour and hitting him head-on. Three miles later, in tiny Bergen, several residents advised him to stop over. So after only sixteen miles—his shortest stint to date—he did stop for the night. Provided he could get in a good day on Friday, he could still reach Buffalo.

What a day that followed! Determined to cover the forty-four miles to Buffalo by Friday evening, Weston breakfasted and left Bergen at 7:30 a.m. It was still snowing with the drifts piling more and more snow and the gale continuing to howl. Chugging twelve miles to Bryan in two hours, Weston had a cup of coffee and some eggs. Plowing onward, he hit a six-foot drift, crawling through it on his hands and knees. "Lots of fun," he kidded in his report, "with no one in sight except a dog." His support car was stuck in a drift, far behind him. Weston trudged along anyway, stopping two miles farther up the road when he felt faint, only to be met by Mr. and Mrs. Fred Blood armed with a refreshing bowl of hot milk—"a lifesaver sure enough." His strength restored, Weston trotted westward into Batavia.

It was a homecoming of sorts, with the route similar to the one he had traveled forty-two years ago on his way from Portland to Chicago. As he neared Batavia, the town's police chief, J. C. McCulley, met Weston, telling him this wasn't the second but the *third* time he had escorted him through the city. Passing through a gauntlet of cheering residents, the two men made their way to the home of former alderman Edward Russell, another old-timer who had accompanied Weston for several miles on that 1867 walk. After a thirty-minute rest, Weston was on his way again for Buffalo, now thirty-six miles away.

Another ordeal lay just ahead. Weston's car and support team were lagging, so the pedestrian relied on local reports to guide his route out of town. Due for a lecture at Shea's Theatre in Buffalo, Weston, accompanied for the day by three fellow walkists, was expected to arrive at 10:30 p.m. But with the snow still falling and the wind whipping up, the roads turned to a combination of slush and mud. Weston was getting knocked this way and that and realized he would never get there in time. So fifteen miles from their destination, the walking party telephoned the theater, explaining to Mr. Shea that their pace slowed to three miles per hour. So they would be late, very late.

Mr. Shea had his own challenges. The theater was packed to the gills, the crowd awaiting Weston. So why couldn't the old pedestrian just mark his spot, hop in his recently arrived car, and head to the theater, Mr. Shea reasoned. He could then retrace his steps and resume his walk the following morning.

Out of the question, Mr. Weston countered. "The idea was absurd, and under no circumstances would I place my foot in a vehicle on a secular day," he said. "Not for any amount of money would I violate the conditions of any walking contract."

So Mr. Shea was out of luck. Most of the crowd stuck around till midnight, hoping Mr. Weston would show, but the old pedestrian was still ten miles from the destination and having a very hard time of it. He never got there that evening. Just east of the colorfully named hamlet of Bowmansville, Weston fell, this time cracking his head on the ice and his left arm taking his weight.

But Providence was again looking down on Weston. Stop now? No way. Energized by the two hundred or so residents who had ventured out several miles from town to meet him, Weston gamely plodded ahead to the Buffalo city line, where a score of policemen, including a dozen mounted officers and the chief of police, Michael Regan, accompanied him all the way downtown. So even if Mr. Shea was miffed that Weston hadn't delivered his lecture at his theater, the locals got over it—showering Weston with a salute to remember. Hitting town well past midnight, fireworks shot off from John Schwalbe's roadhouse, and residents thronged the route. Later, at the handsome Iroquois Hotel, the hotel physician tended to his injuries.

The good doctor did his best, tending to Weston until 5:00 a.m. But the old pedestrian couldn't sleep. Treating himself to a generous breakfast, Weston felt better. On Saturday's agenda was a forty-five-mile jaunt south toward Pennsylvania to Machias, where he would remain Sunday and rest up.

There was a reason New York's baseball teams were still in the south, only now preparing to head north for their home openers in early April. In the north, foul weather still raged—and that Saturday, March 28, in Dallas, John McGraw's New York Giants, behind pitcher Rube Marquard, toyed with its Texas League farm club, the Dallas Giants, winning 9–1. In the meantime, the Americans, soon to be called the Yankees, were in Macon, Georgia, where they tended to a lineup that featured Hall of Famer Willie Keeler, for an exhibition game Sunday against the South Atlantic League's Columbus Foxes. Meanwhile, in southwestern New York, the prospect of the coming baseball seasoned still seemed far, far away, as Weston struggled with roads he described as having "the hardest, deepest, and toughest mud."

Weston gamely carried on anyway, slogging thirty-four miles to a town called Paradise, which on this day was anything but. It was there at 11:00 p.m., still sixteen miles short of his destination of Machias, that the pedestrian got an offer he couldn't refuse. All day Weston had fought the elements, forced at several spots to tramp through the fields to avoid the deep drifts on the road. He did this all by himself since the car had stalled again, this time in a snowbank. Fortunately, residents along the way plied him with enough hot coffee and eggs and milk to satisfy the old pedestrian's gnawing hunger.

The offer of offers came toward the end of a hard day from a couple of those Good Samaritans, R. L. Willis and Jesse Ward. It couldn't have been more timely—a comfortable place to stay for the next couple of evenings in exchange for a couple of lectures. Weston accepted on the spot—"a most agreeable surprise," he called the chance meeting—so to nearby Chafee he went for some R & R. That Sunday, he lectured not once or twice but three times—in nearby Arcade and Yorkshire Corners and in Olean, where he spoke to the town's Snowshoe Club. The timing was auspicious, giving him both a much-needed mental break and time to heal. And just like that, Weston was basking in the warmth of new friends and the satisfaction that he had somehow trekked 249 miles during the week, a daily average the last six days of 41 miles a day in wretched conditions. That put the old pedestrian 522 miles into his trip across America, about one-sixth of the way to San Francisco.

. . .

Weston was pleased as punch to speak at the Olean Snowshoe Club, where he enjoyed honorary membership as did former president Theodore Roosevelt and New York governor Charles Evans Hughes. Arguably, Weston felt most comfortable in the small towns like the ones in western New York, where schools and business let out just to see him stride by and factory whistles heralded his appearance. More intimate than New York City or Rochester, these were places where Weston could really chat with residents and pose for photos, sometimes with half the town's population. And they seldom attracted the crush of crowds that could cause him to turn an ankle. Not that Weston was ever for a moment out of the public eye; between the crowds turned out to see him and the daily reports back to the *New York Times*, Weston on his great 1909 trek across America was in the public eye more than ever.

An article on Sunday, March 28, in the *Syracuse Herald* that was headlined "Is a Grand Old Man" was written as if there really wasn't a need to include his last name. Grand Old Man? That must be Weston. Yes, it was, and the piece revealed what a lot of people were thinking: "(Weston)'s a study," the paper wrote, "this little old man who defies time and the elements when he sets himself a task, as he plods along with his queer little running walk, mile after mile, hour after hour, day after day, undeterred, undismayed, no matter what confronts him."

The *Herald* attributed three sources to his success, starting with its early twentieth-century comprehension of genetics. "He comes from a long line of God-fearing New England ancestors, who, as far as he knows, were free from blood or organic diseases," the newspaper wrote. His superb constitution and indomitable will as well as his "instinctive knowledge of hygiene" were the other factors. Then the *Herald* delved into a detailed discourse of Weston's "marvelous stomach," which "digests whatever he puts in it." That would be chops, steaks, roasts, fish, eggs, potatoes, all sorts of vegetables, cereals, tea, coffee, milk, fruit of all sorts, as well as prunes. "He is an advocate of prunes," the paper added. "They are the only laxative he knows."

The *Times* included its own insights that Sunday about Weston's health. "The explanation of his superb condition lies simply in the regularity of his habits and the simplicity of the fare that he eats," it wrote. "While not a total abstainer either from liquor or tobacco, he is an excessively temperate man."

Did any other athlete of the age attract such scrutiny about their training regimens? People analyzed Ty Cobb's choked-up batting stance and Christy Mathewson's "out" pitch, his celebrated fadeaway, but seldom their diets. With Weston, everything was up for inspection as if we were a science experiment. Weston drank, but never in a bar, the *Times* reported. His food choices were nutritious—modest, heavy on the carbohydrates, seldom rich, and built for sustenance. After nearly a half century of walking, Weston knew what worked best for him and what didn't—and that meant abstaining from anything upsetting his stomach and absolutely no pastries.

All those decades of walking had given Weston a lot of time to think about the lifestyle that best suited him. Daily naps worked for the seventy-year-old man, particularly right after a meal. Six hours of sleep a night were plenty; any more left him lethargic the following day. Weston had never been seriously ill in his adult years, save an 1871 attack of typhoid; and like former president Roosevelt, he had become a living testament to the benefits of overcoming a sickly childhood with exercise. The best way of combating a cold and other minor ailments? Sweat them out with exercise, Weston counseled, and you'll feel better in a day.

"Weston, in spite of his gray hairs, gives one the impression of much less an age than he really is, and his vitality and wiry vigor are astounding," the *Times* reported. "The usual deterioration which is noticeable in men of seventy years of age, in the tissues and blood vessels, is entirely lacking in him."

Not surprisingly, many of Weston's most ardent admirers were physicians. Taking on Dr. Osler's theories of old age, as Weston had done in Yonkers, Dr. Frederic Brush, the superintendent of the New York Post-Graduate Medical School and Hospital, said the old pedestrian's greatest gift was in "convincing other men that they are capable of a great deal more than they now think."

For Brush, Weston was a role model. "You know how men so often nowadays begin to let things slip at about forty-five and then at fifty give up altogether?" the doctor asked. "It's a reaction against this that I hope will follow Weston's extraordinary example. It should bring more energy all around; more energy in exercising, more energy in business. It should make these adherents of the misnamed 'Osler theory' . . . courageous and cheerful. If the Weston enterprise can do that, and it certainly tends to, he will have done something greater than to excite the astonishment and admiration of the country—that he has done already."

Manhattan physician, Dr. Henry S. Pascal, was a particular admirer. "An example to other men middle age, he certainly is that," the good doctor said of Weston. "He is a natural exception, yet I think he does show to a large degree what other men might be. He has simply by diet and moderation and exercise kept himself young." Only Dr. J. Leonard Corning, a nerve specialist, provided anything less that universal praise. Though opposed to excessive exercise, he called Weston "an edifying spectacle," a kind of freak of nature whose powers were "largely, very largely" inherited. "Few, if any, men could be at his age in such a condition of strength," he said. Nonetheless, "he is an example of remarkable vitality."

. . .

On Monday, March 29, Edward Payson Weston kicked off week three of his Great Walk to the Pacific by trekking thirty-three miles from Chaffee to Olean, where he ate a light supper and delivered a lecture that evening to eighteen hundred people at the Opera House. It snowed, but the weather had held up and the roads remained relatively firm—fortunate news for Weston, who wrenched his ankle on the way. On the surface, it seemed like a largely uneventful day.

Hardly. Nearly six hundred miles into his walk, Weston was the talk of western New York, where big crowds, not only in cities and towns but in the smallest of hamlets, were turning out to see him. The time didn't matter: leaving Chaffee *at 3:30 a.m.*, Weston drew a crowd more interested in accompanying him the two miles to Yorkshire than in sleeping. The chance to say they had walked with the greatest walker of the age was the equivalent of playing catch with Honus Wagner. Weston reveled in the adulation, gushing that "the enthusiasm along my route is beyond description." Police escorts through town had become standard procedure, and so had the factory whistles, ringing church bells, and brass bands. Weston's great trek west had become a moving parade, rural America's 1909 version of Beatlemania. "One cannot imagine how light-hearted and gay these demonstrations make me," the old pedestrian said.

On Monday, schools in Machias were dismissed in honor of Weston's visit. Many of the seventy schoolchildren went to the road to see him walk past on his way to Franklinville. But when some children decided to accompany him, Weston urged them to turn back, concerned they could be caught in the snow, and probably to preserve his heels. "I . . . thought it best to remind the children that it would seem a longer distance on their walk homeward," he said. All but six girls did. What to do? Weston had them to lunch.

Another twenty miles down the road, the tiny town of Hinsdale rolled out all the stops, greeting Weston with a brass band and a gaggle of well-wishers, most of whom shook his hand at lunch. All day long the plaudits continued, a rolling celebration of Weston and his great walk. At the Reynolds' family farm, two young girls greeted the old pedestrian by singing, "Glory, Glory, Hallelujah, Weston Is Marching On." Then another brass band met him in Olean. The attention suited a profoundly social person.

So did the weather, at last. Walking Tuesday, March 31, some fifty-one miles west to Jamestown, New York, warming temperatures had set Weston in a buoyant mood. Sure, there was mud—lots of the oozy, cakey variety. But the pleasant rolling hills of the wonderfully named Big Brokenstraw Valley and the welcoming crowds were comforting, as was the knowledge that the pedestrian could be in Ohio by week's end. For now, the plan was to get to a lecture at the YMCA in Jamestown, before heading south through Meadville, Pennsylvania, on the way to another lecture in Pittsburgh, then spelled "Pittsburg."

So anxious were many to meet the great pedestrian that people were heading farther and farther from the town centers to meet him. Weston had left Olean at 4:00 a.m., which he figured was plenty of time to reach Jamestown for his lecture at about 10:00 p.m. But slowed late in the afternoon by muddy roads between Salamanca and Randolph to a pace of no more than three miles per hour, he had fallen well behind schedule. Then, about four miles east of Jamestown, some two hundred YMCA members and six sturdy policemen were there to escort him to town. By the time Weston reached the YMCA, some eight hundred more—one thousand cheering spectators in all—were there as well. Twenty minutes later the old pedestrian delivered his lecture to the latest and greatest, "most enthusiastic audience I ever addressed."

At 6:30 a.m. on Tuesday, March 31, Weston left Jamestown for Union City, Pennsylvania, some forty-five miles away. His car did not. The mud had slowed up the pedestrian and completely stalled the car ten miles from Jamestown. Weston could find a meal or lodging in the cities, but not having access to supplies from his car was a big deal on remote stretches of road where the seventy-year-old pedestrian found himself famished or faint and reliant on Good Samaritans. Weston's car stored his coveted bread from a friend, Adolph Schinkel, a baker from Ninth Avenue in New York, along with beef extracts as well as spare clothing and extra shoes. "The absence of these necessities inconvenienced me greatly and to some extent impeded progress," Weston said. For weeks, Weston's car traumas would be a continuing saga. Could a horse-drawn wagon have been more dependable after all?

That Wednesday, April 1, during his thirty-mile trek from Union City to Meadville, Pennsylvania, Weston would have appreciated a horse-drawn wagon. Thank goodness for all those Good Samaritans like C. E. Mandaville, who on Tuesday had accompanied Weston from Clymer, New York, to Union City. Another was N. R. Allen, who the next morning, some two hours south of Union City, New York, helped revive a feeble-looking pedestrian with coffee and a timely slab of homemade cake. On Thursday in Cambridge Springs, about halfway to Meadville, one William Baird served as a guardian angel by delivering Weston with a comfortable bed *and* hot applications for his arm, still sore from the previous week's fall. Heartened and greatly relieved by the chance meetings, Weston admitted how badly he needed his support team. He couldn't be counting on all those Samaritans in remote areas of the West.

Also that Wednesday, somewhere between Weston's bottomless cups of coffee and the hot applications for his arm, U.S. Army sergeant John Walsh sauntered into Boston, having trekked 7,770 miles from Boston to San Francisco and back again in 156 days. Walsh, who had dropped fifty pounds on the trip, was a spry fifty-seven years old and apparently a man itching to get back on the road. Distributing a statement and a press release in Boston, he immediately took off again for San Francisco, looking to peel off another there and back. The feat was impressive, even awesome, but merited all of a paragraph in the next day's *New York Times* under the headline, "Another Transcontinental Walker." Next to Edward Payson Weston, Sergeant John Walsh was just another walker.

.

5

"I Will Not Alter My Mode of Travel!"

Bounding off the steps of the State House in Boston on February 22, 1861, on his way to Washington DC, Edward Payson Weston set off down Beacon Street at such a clip that few could keep up with him. Considering the number of creditors looking to delay his trip, it's no wonder the twenty-two-year-old New Englander was anxious to be moving.

Constable A. G. Dawes had been the first impediment, present at the send-off, not to cheer Weston or keep order, but to serve a claim for a debt. Another man, D. F. Draper, was there as well, saying that Weston owed him too. Weston argued he was penniless but, after heated negotiations, agreed to pay his debts upon his return. He had already won over the crowd—"Shame on them," several of Weston's supporters roared at the creditors. And then he was off, trailed by dozens of fans who could barely keep the pace. Within a few blocks, they gave up. Weston blazed those first five miles in forty-seven minutes—faster than many could *run* it—before settling down a little to a steady gait of three and a half miles per hour.

Seventeen miles into his first great walk, a company of parading soldiers serenaded Weston at Natick with three cheers and by presenting arms. Bowing in grateful acknowledgment, the spry pedestrian kept moving and ambled another four miles into Framingham, where a group of drummers escorted him to the Framingham Hotel. There Weston and his party were fed after being led into the dining room to meet a group of women. Asked by one woman to deliver a kiss to the president, Weston gave back as good as he got. He could make no guarantees about the delivery, he retorted, but had no objections if the woman—or anyone else in the party—cared to give *him* a kiss.

It wasn't apparent at the time, but a half day into his first substantial trek Weston was already creating a pattern for the next half century of walking. His blend of athleticism mixed with theatrical touches would become a blueprint for the look, feel, grit, pathos, and humor of future walks. Thanking his hosts in Framingham, Weston delivered a brief speech to a crowd gathered outside; and accompanied by many of the villagers and those persistent drummers, he bounded off to Worcester, twenty-four miles west.

If the attention surprised Weston, he never let on. A ham at heart with pinpoint timing to deliver funny lines on demand, Weston was up for it. Three miles later a carriage containing a man and two women pulled up alongside the pedestrian, having ridden ten miles just to shake hands and wish him well. Tramping through Westborough, Weston was informed by a young man that he had bet twenty dollars that he would make it to Washington, hoping the pedestrian would arrive in Washington DC on time, to which Weston laughed out loud. Things went swimmingly until Weston's past again caught up with him outside Worcester, where a certain Mr. Balcom accompanied by the county sheriff pulled up in a carriage to inform him that he would be arrested at the city line for not paying his debts. Onward, the party headed into town to the Lincoln House Hotel, where Weston scraped out of trouble, yet again, by pledging to pay Mr. Balcom after the trip.

The walkist had already covered close to forty miles, meeting his first-day goal. So was it time then for a rest? Not yet. So pumped up that he couldn't sleep, Weston left the Lincoln

House Hotel just past 2:00 a.m. and walked another six miles through twelve-inch-deep snows to Leicester. Finally, Weston really was beat. Growing dizzy and having trouble keeping his eyes open, he fell several times, and his nose began bleeding. *That* woke him up; and arriving at dawn in Leicester, Weston took a break at last and headed to a local hotel for a bath and a nap. Close to fifty miles into his journey to Washington DC, he was finally at rest.

An hour later Weston sat up and felt fully refreshed. Why wait? Grabbing a bag of fresh doughnuts, Weston marched another eight miles to the Wawconnuck Hotel in East Brunswick, where he had a real breakfast and a rubdown, and took off again by midday. The credit went to one of Weston's true gifts from the gods, his smoothly working metabolism and body type that enabled him to rest for short periods and feel as fresh as if he had slept an entire night. It also gave Weston the advantage of dividing his walks not into twenty-four-hour increments but into more convenient two-, three-, and four-hour segments, or however long it took for Weston to make it to lunch or to the next hotel or small-town ceremony.

Weston was a quick study, a sponge for learning on the go, and incorporated what worked and not what didn't. Just beyond West Warren, Massachusetts, where he was presented with an American flag and a seven-gun salute, an elderly man asked if he could walk with him awhile. It would slow him down, but Weston readily agreed, realizing that the benefits were worth the effort. For every elderly walker who slowed him down were five or ten fit locals eager to walk with Weston at the edge of town and provide the local scuttlebutt on where to eat and stay, what roads to take, and what dogs to avoid. It was the Victorian era's version of social media, and Weston was quick to reciprocate. Hotel operators offering Weston free lodging became fast friends; the pedestrian would often mention their names and establishments to reporters in a kind of unspoken quid pro quo. That also went for farmers and residents, whom Weston called out in print, lavishing praise on those who had offered him coffee or a place to nap.

Weston kept timetables and soon learned to factor in a few minutes here and there for ceremonies and unexpected encounters. Also, he was learning to use his intuition in choosing the best routes, highways for the most part; but he would use another route as well if a local suggested it. On this trip, Weston would make his way largely along the old Boston Post Road, originally a system of mail-delivery routes between Boston and New York that evolved into the first major highway in the United States. Finding his way to other historical trails would be a pattern Weston would follow throughout his career, from the old Mohawk or Iroquois Trails across upstate New York to the Mormon Trail through Illinois and other parts of the Midwest all the way to Utah.

The rubdown in New Brunswick worked its magic. So on Sunday, February 24, in Palmer, Massachusetts, Weston had another and would incorporate them into his regular training regimen. Walking burned calories and could make him very hungry very quickly, so Weston learned to rely on the many offerings from spectators and home owners along the way. And he quickly discovered what foods worked best: milk, water, and loaves of bread became his staples, placing the pedestrian at the forefront of endurance athletes who recognize the benefits of bland carbo-loading and energy-restoring nourishment. Struck from the list were sandwiches coated with mustard, which Weston once consumed on a walk through New Jersey, causing him a severe stomachache.

Given the delays, it's remarkable just how many people waited *for hours* along the roads and in towns just to see this young walking man. Newspaper articles and word of mouth gave people an idea of when he was expected to be in the area, but a bout of illness or trouble with snow could leave him significantly time challenged. On February 28, en route to Washington DC, Weston was due in Trenton, New Jersey, where city officials had pegged him as the main attraction of a grand reception. But deep snows on roads out of New Brunswick had slowed "the walkist," as Weston had become known, and caused him to turn his ankle. Refusing to be driven to Trenton, he soldiered on to a tavern in tiny Clarksville, seven miles from his goal. Seriously weary, Weston could think of little beyond taking a deep sleep, so to bed he went for six glorious and badly needed hours, all the way to the morning of Friday, March 1. Trenton would have to wait.

Weston got there later—not until late Friday morning. On his way across the Delaware River and bounding into Pennsylvania by afternoon, Weston was in Philadelphia by nightfall. Pumped up by a pleasant reception on arriving at the Continental Hotel in Philadelphia at 8:15 p.m., Weston bounded up the stairs to his room, refusing to use the new steam elevator. "As I commenced to walk," he said, "I will not alter my mode of travel until I arrive in Washington!"

On Monday, March 4, Inauguration Day in Washington was a day away, and Weston found himself traipsing through northern Maryland with time vanishing and slate-gray skies promising more snow. Another knotty problem was numerous tollgates, which a gatekeeper had to open. Though some keepers were there, others were not, delaying him. Reaching the Eutaw Hotel in Baltimore at 4:30 a.m., Weston and his company were seriously famished and badly needed a meal. Not a problem, said the proprietor, Robert Coleman, who fired up the stove to deliver a memorable meal in a hurry. Weston was back on the road by 6:00 a.m. with a day and several hours left to cover the final forty miles to Washington.

The walkist was down to the wire. The snow came heavily and kept clogging the roads. The temperatures continued to drop as the winds howled. Outside Washington Junction,

Maryland, thirty miles from the U.S. Capitol, the horse pulling Weston's carriage got ornery and refused to go a step farther. Walking into town, Weston tried to secure another horse but found none available. Returning to his party, the pedestrian suggested his comrades hop aboard a train for the final leg to Washington DC; he would trek the rest of the way alone.

So he did, arriving in Washington late in the morning of Tuesday, March 5, accompanied by an appreciative crowd. He had trekked 510 miles in ten days, four hours, and twelve minutes through deep snow—just four hours and twelve minutes past the inauguration deadline. Admitting he was "somewhat tired," Weston found a police officer who directed him to a rooming house, where he ate and had a long sleep. All that effort and the pedestrian had lost his bet. Or had he? Walking to Washington had made him a celebrity.

Weston slept a fitful ten hours and arose on Wednesday, March 6, to declare he had "never felt better." Visiting the Capitol, he ran into Rep. Christopher Robinson of his native Rhode Island, who introduced him to a number of other government officials. Among them was the powerful senator from Illinois Stephen Douglas, who took a liking to the young pedestrian and, some days later, introduced him to another Illinois politician: President Lincoln. Impressed by his accomplishment, the new president offered to pay the costs of Weston's trip home. The plucky pedestrian wouldn't hear of it, vowing to walk the 510 miles back to Boston—and this time, in ten days.

That prompted the president to compare Weston to a Native American wagon wheel, because "he was never tired." But before he could even leave Washington, Weston's plans changed abruptly. With the nation on the verge of Civil War and tens of thousands of troops already in uniform, Weston agreed to put his pedestrian skills to the test by delivering to U.S. soldiers a series of letters derailed by a recent anti-Union riot in Baltimore. On this walk, Weston succeeded; he managed to get all

117 letters to soldiers of the Massachusetts and New York regiments stationed south of the Mason-Dixon Line in Annapolis, Maryland. Doing so took pluck, luck, some daring, and a touch of élan. Tucking the letters deep inside his garments, Weston went undercover with a series of aliases, pretending to be everything from a beggar to a woodcutter to a sixteen-year-old orphan. Even the soldiers to whom he delivered the letters were fooled; and not believing he was who he said he was, they arrested Weston before the order came down to let him go.

Weston would forever be proud of his military service. But his failure to get from Boston to the inauguration in ten days gnawed at him. Delayed by creditors and all that snow, Weston knew he could have easily reached the deadline in optimal conditions. "I never have made it a rule to commence anything and leave it 'half done,'" he said. "I deem it a . . . duty to 'try it again'; inasmuch, as some persons have intimated that I could have made up the lost time, if I had not been hired to do otherwise, or in other words, it was policy for me to arrive in Washington too late to gain the wager." He resolved to retrace his steps—and this time, in those ten days. Weston didn't leave for more than a year, enabling him to pay off creditors and wait for better conditions. Taking off May 19, 1862, in pleasant spring temperatures and on dirt-hardened roads, Weston wended back to Boston, not in ten days, but in *eight*. Weston had proven something to himself and to everyone else: at twenty-three, he had already become America's greatest pedestrian.

6

"The People Treat Me Finely"

Preparing to leave Meadville, Pennsylvania, in the gloomy dawn of the morning of Friday, April 2, 1909, and head forty-five miles to the town of Sharon, Edward Payson Weston faced a series of challenges.

The claylike mud was knee-deep in places.

The car was still missing.

Then the lecture he was due to give in Pittsburgh had been cancelled.

But Weston was in a chipper mood. And for the moment, at least, he wasn't letting the realities bother him. Mud? An occupational hazard. Though it caked him almost daily, it was April, which promised the arrival of warmer days, dirt-packed roads, and sun. Even baseball season was just ahead. The AWOL car? Weston was already used to the breakdowns. Last spotted early Wednesday at the YMCA in Jamestown, New York, the car was stalled for now in a mud hole between Waterford, Pennsylvania, and Cambridge Springs. For the time being, Weston would make do without his trainers, driver, vehicle, and supplies. And skipping Pittsburgh just may have been a blessing in disguise; it meant Weston could turn west more quickly to make up for delays he had encountered with the snows of New York.

Weston had planned on heading to Pittsburgh as a pledge

to friends. But the speaking session there fell through, which was just as well because it would have added another one hundred miles and an extra two days to his trek. But that was only part of the story. A marathon was scheduled in Pittsburgh at the same time Weston was supposed to be there, creating what would have been a case of bad timing in the extreme. As he had demonstrated in Yonkers, the old pedestrian had turned his loathing of marathons into a central part of his lectures. "I am against these heart-rending marathon races," Weston bluntly told his readers in the *New York Times*, "and would certainly say something against them had I gone to Pittsburgh."

So on April 1 Weston rambled those forty-five miles to Sharon—some seventy-five miles north of Pittsburgh—enabling him to get within two miles of the Ohio border. From the start of his walk day at 6:00 a.m., Weston encountered slippery clay roads oozing with frost that compromised his footing. "The . . . miles I walked . . . did not consume one-fifth the strength or one-half the exertion it did to walk the first seven miles to Sharon," Weston said. "Placing my right foot a little ahead, it would slip back six or eight inches before you could get the left foot located, which in its turn would try to slide off into another county, leaving me to look after it."

Weston's thighs still took a beating. But there he was at 7:00 p.m., arriving in Sharon, feeling fit, and following up on Saturday with an easy fourteen miles into a day's rest at the Todd House in Youngstown, Ohio. After three weeks, Weston had trekked 748 miles across America, generating headlines nearly every day. A barometer of the interest was Weston's daily dispatch in the *Times*, which continued to earn prominent space at the expense of marathons, which were being run here, there, and everywhere. "Weston Is Cheered by Great Crowds" headlined the pedestrian's Monday, April 5, *Times* report from Youngstown. The six-graph story that featured a mileage chart of his trip ran in the paper's top left-hand corner of page 8 over two columns, next to a shorter article about Saturday's marathon at the Polo Grounds in New York. From all accounts, the marathon was quite the race—Henri St. Yves of France beat Hayes and Pietri in what would "do much toward keeping alive the public interest in the sport," the *Times* wrote. But in the court of public acclaim, those marathoners didn't measure up to the mania generated by one Edward Payson Weston.

. . .

From the hustle and bustle of America's biggest metropolis, Weston had reached the industrial heart of Ohio. Cutting a path through the center of the state promised bigger towns, bigger crowds, and more opportunity to earn extra income with lectures. From the steel center of Youngstown, Weston planned to head west and slightly south through Canton, then more directly west through Wooster and Mansfield, and then northwest into Toledo.

Weston took off at five minutes after midnight on Monday, April 5, from Youngstown, looking to make it to Canton, fifty-six miles due west. The police captain and officers were there to escort Weston to the city limits. So was a pumped-up nighttime crowd of a hundred or so, including one Ralph Stewart, a seventeen-year-old Johnstown, Pennsylvania, native who boldly announced he intended to accompany the great pedestrian all the way to San Francisco. Young Stewart seemed focused— prompting the question of how exactly he had made it from Johnstown, Pennsylvania, more than one hundred miles west, to Youngstown. Had he walked? Taken a train? The question was lost in the moment as the teenager and his older companion plowed some twenty miles southwest to Salem, gathering attention, applause, and newspaper coverage along the way. But in Salem, reality caught up with the youngster. Spent, Stewart went no farther, deciding he couldn't reach Canton, let alone San Francisco, and disappeared into history.

Not that the seventy-year-old pedestrian needed the company. Hitting Salem at 6:45 a.m., Weston breakfasted and was on his way in a half hour. More than thirty-five miles of walking for the day still remained, and Weston was anxious to reach Canton by late afternoon. A big reception awaited him there, and it would be even bigger provided he could get there in daylight. And he was due to lecture there that evening. So all day, Weston plodded at a steady gait, encouraged by solid roads; and after only one more stop, he made it to Canton.

Canton's city officials were ready. For some reason, Weston hadn't visited the area since giving a demonstration of walking at the Stark County Fair thirty-eight years before, in 1871. In between, a lot had happened there: the city had given birth both to American professional football and to one of the sport's first great teams, the Canton Bulldogs. The city knew how to treat its sports heroes. For days, the pedestrian's presence had been eagerly anticipated; on Saturday, the *Evening Independent* of Massillon, west of Canton, had trumpeted Weston's impending arrival with its lead piece chock full of exuberant praise and the news that the "champion walker of the world" would soon be there. "It is expected that the roads will be lined with spectators," the paper gushed of his visit, describing Weston's transcontinental walk as "the greatest which he has ever undertaken and one which will find no parallel among the feats of all living walkers of his age." It was 5:10 p.m. Monday when Weston, right on schedule, strolled by the home of Canton's most famous native son, former president William McKinley, and on down Lake and North Market Streets into the center of town.

An old-fashioned hoedown, a bona fide outpouring of affection for America's most popular septuagenarian, was set for Canton. More than five thousand people lined the streets of Canton as Weston marked his triumphant entry by smiling broadly and blowing kisses to women. He was the man of the hour with no one caring a hoot for his eccentric wardrobe of leather leggings bound nearly up to his knees with light checkered trousers, a shirt with necktie wrapped in a blue serge coat, and a floppy straw hat. Others looked on from cars and carriages, honking horns, whistling, and shouting their greetings. Some followed him, or rather they followed the protective shell of patrolmen and city officials who formed a barricade around the old pedestrian as he neared the Courtland Hotel, his destination for the evening. "Not since the days of McKinley . . . had the county seat seen such a demonstration as took place Monday afternoon when Edward Payson Weston, aged seventy-one, veteran pedestrian and lecturer, on his tramp from New York to San Francisco, reached the city," wrote the *Evening Independent.*

By the time Weston reached the hotel, the crowd had surged to fifteen thousand, including a special reception committee who wore badges with the inscription, "Canton Welcomes Weston." Committee members had done their homework, bringing to town a seventy-seven-year-old Akron resident named W. E. Merriman, who had seen Weston forty-two years before on his 1867 trek through Cleveland from Portland to Chicago. Merriman said he had hitched up a horse that long-ago day and traveled from Akron to Cleveland just to walk with the great Weston for a spell. He even produced a photo from that long-ago day of the two men together. Reuniting in the lobby of the Courtland, the two white-haired senior citizens swapped stories about the old days. Then Weston bounded up the stairs to the hotel balcony for a short address of thanks to the solid mass of humanity who filled the square outside the hotel. All in all, this reception, he claimed, had outdone any he had experienced so far on his trip.

. . .

The rains that Weston had been fortunate to avoid thus far in Ohio returned Tuesday morning with a vengeance. It poured as if the heavens had let loose their own tribute to the old pedestrian. But with the cheers of the Cantonians still ringing in his ears and the prospect of two new young pedestrians vowing to walk with him the thirty-four miles to Wooster, Weston was in buoyant spirits. And he was ready to roll.

The skies opened up just east of Massillon, but the old pedestrian was prepared. With the car still in the shop, Weston had hired a horse-drawn carriage to carry his supplies, so he was able to slip into his oilskin coat and cap. With the skies dropping buckets, Weston ran into an intrepid reporter from the *Evening Independent*, ever mindful that the great man's every move in and around Massillon was a big story. "Howdy do?" Weston greeted the reporter, barely seeming to acknowledge the soaking rain. What followed was a virtual transcript of their conversation, providing a splendid rendering of the state of mind of the great pedestrian some eight hundred miles into his great trek across America.

On Tuesday, April 6, 1909, in central Ohio, Weston was most concerned that his rainfall ensemble—a rubber coat, high-laced boots, oilskin hat, and riding breeches—would be enough to keep him dry. With water falling from his drooping white mustache and his boots slathered in mud—what else was new?—Weston focused on how the weight of his watery jacket had slowed him down to steps with shorter, jerkier motions. The jacket was "as heavy as lead and as hot as fire," the walkist lamented.

But Weston was chipper that soggy morning, energized by the reception at a convent school whose students had poured to the edge of the property and cheered as he passed. "I tell you, they were nice girls, every one of them," the pedestrian said. "I just hoped when I saw them that they would never land in New York; for if there was ever a den of iniquity, there it is."

Working to steer Weston to the subject of his career, the reporter was successful for a minute or so. The pedestrian preferred to chat about his interest . . . in journalism. It had been decades since his newspaper days in New York, but Weston still considered himself every inch the reporter, stating "it was terrible the way [the editors] grind you." But as quickly as that thought was out, Weston was back on the subject of those women of the convent he had passed a few minutes ago. "Here's a good rule to follow," he said. "Treat every young girl and married woman as if she were your sister and you'll never come to grief."

Passing the elegant residence of the Vinedale family, Weston called it a "fine home" and wondered how much it was worth. Reaching the outskirts of Massillon, he met his first knot of locals, newsboys who had finished their morning duties and gone to meet the great man. "Hello, sonnies," Weston called out. "Keep away from my heels."

The newsboys complied. Some fell in behind the pedestrian and followed at a safe distance into town. Others walked by his side, content to gaze on the first national celebrity they had likely ever seen. "The people treat me finely," said Weston, enjoying the company. "Take Ohio people and they are certainly hospitable." Heading down East Main Street toward the hotel, Weston basked in the kind of reception that never got old. Frequently pulling off his oilskin hat to salute the crowds that filled windows and porches of homes along the way, he stopped to kiss the hand of a little girl carrying an American flag. Amid swarms of residents, Weston barely broke stride in going straight to a hotel room where a piece of white toast and a cup of tea awaited him.

The snack hit the spot, prompting Weston to launch into a detailed analysis of his dietary habits. What the great pedestrian ate and imbibed in on his great trek was a frequent topic of interest for journalists meeting him along the way, as it was for readers of the *Times*, which had taken to printing letters from readers wanting to know more about Weston's secrets of success. "I am very much interested in the wonderful exhibition of vitality which is being shown by E. P. Weston, and have seen . . . many allusions to his clean, healthy life, benefits of exercise, 'water wagon' for staying power, etc.," one J. Carr of New York had written in a letter to the paper published the previous Sunday. "Is Mr. Weston a total abstainer from alcohol? If Weston is an abstainer, it would convince many of us who still doubt that alcohol is absolutely unnecessary that we're better off without it."

The question had been passed along to Weston, who was more than happy to hold forth about his diet and alcohol consumption. Weston imbibed moderately, he said, but not so much as a drop beginning a month before a walk and until he was finished. Weston said he never, ever drank at bars, with his only indulgence a California claret during the summer at dinner and an occasional beer while visiting friends in New York.

The concept of a public figure swearing off anything stronger than a beer was unusual in Weston's day. Decades before Alcoholics Anonymous, drinking colossal amounts of alcohol was probably more socially accepted and evident at every level of society. That was certainly the case in New York, where booze flowed freely—"from the beer halls in the immigrant quarters of the Lower East Side to the clubs and moneyed nightlife farther uptown," as the *New York Times* put it in a 2012 review of Richard Zack's book *Island of Vice*, which chronicles Theodore Roosevelt's tenure heading the board of the city's police commissioners. Roosevelt led the police department from 1895 to 1897 and did his blustery best to claim what he called an urban culture run amuck—one claiming eight thousand saloons for a population of 2.5 million. Today in New York, there are more bars—just above ten thousand according to the New York State Liquor Authority—but the city is vastly bigger in land mass and more than three times as populous. Detailed in Zack's book are enough alcohol-infused tales of Gilded Age debauchery and excess to make a rock star blush. At one such party attended by the architect Stanford White, thirty-three people downed 144 bottles of champagne just before a thinly clad sixteen-year-old girl emerged from an oversized cake.

Weston was one of the era's few notable athletes to fully embrace the concept of foods as fuel and refraining from alcohol. Baseball players were among the era's most notorious drinkers, some of whom had met unfortunate ends as a result. Fresh on the minds of readers of the sports pages in 1909 was the tragic death of the great slugger "Big" Ed Delahanty, which occurred six years before under murky details at Niagara Falls. Tossed off a train for drinking and threatening passengers with a razor, Big Ed was making his way across the International Railway Bridge, from which he either fell or jumped. The tragedy underscored baseball's complex relationship with alcohol, which ironically mixed the drunkenness of many players and the professional leagues' tendency to avoid scheduling games on Sunday in deference to the Sabbath. Even so, brewery heads owned many of the big-league teams and were more than willing to peddle their product to patrons. Baseball was so saturated with alcohol that the Philadelphia A's owner and manager Connie Mack, a teetotaler in deference to his mother, famously declared that "Old Man Booze has put more men out of the game than all the umpires together." His comments would be lifted and made into placards adopted by the Pennsylvania Woman's Christian Temperance Union.

Weston recognized the dangers of alcohol. At home he often joined his baker Adolph Schinkel for beer and cards. But he drank moderately, splitting a single growler, or bottle of beer, and never overdoing it. At the dining room table, Weston generally stuck to two meals a day with a single daily helping of meat. Breakfast was his heartiest helping of the day, fortifying him for exercise with a large but precise array of food: a plate of oatmeal and milk, two large slices of the homemade bread with three poached eggs, and another slice of buttered bread, topped off by two cups of coffee and fruit. Dinner was moderate and carefully chosen: a bowl of vegetable soup, a hamburger or two meatballs, mashed potatoes, macaroni, spinach, bread and butter, rice pudding, and one or two cups of tea.

. . .

Weston had stopped in Massillon for several reasons. His attendants, now a twosome, had finally shown up—arriving by train with the car still in the shop and delivering his long-lost extra supplies: three pairs of boots, a dozen pairs of socks, ample underclothes, two dozen handkerchiefs, two white garibaldis, an oilskin coat, and a straw hat. So at the hotel, the old pedestrian removed his drenched clothing, stretched out on a sofa and had a massage. After changing into dry underwear, he strapped a rubber covering over his legs. Next, he exchanged wet shoes for dry ones and vowed to get back to his previous routine of alternating footwear every three days.

With that, Weston was just about set to resume his trek to Wooster with all the details of his ninety-minute stop in Massillon recorded for posterity by the correspondent from the *Evening Independent.* Descending the hotel stairs backward to save stress on his leg muscles, he sauntered through the lobby and into the westward-bound street, where more crowds awaited him. Police Chief Edward Ertle led the way, shooing away anyone who might nip Weston's heel.

Weston needed to make good time to Wooster, where he was due to lecture that evening. From there he was planning to strike into western Ohio and Indiana, reaching Chicago by April 16 or 17. From Chicago, Weston wasn't certain of the kinds of roads he would encounter, but he had been given the assurance of officials of the Southern Pacific Railroad that its section hands and railroad workers would help him. And though many doubted Weston at seventy could get to California, the great pedestrian himself had no doubt he would make it—stating he expected to reach San Francisco on July 8. After that was when Weston *really* planned to get to work and hit the lecture circuit for a month. Do that, he said, and he could clear $10,000.

The pedestrian covered the day's remaining twenty-nine miles without a break. The rain stopped at 4:00 p.m., and ninety minutes later Weston was in Wooster, met by a throng of townspeople. With him were a couple of fellow walkers, one of whom, Robert Rede, had walked with him all the way from Canton. But it was Weston's other companion, thirteen-year-old Cletus Wampler, who had trekked from Massillon to Wooster and earned the old pedestrian's enduring admiration. Wampler was a "bright lad" who walked "bravely" while refusing several rides along the way, he said. Those words of praise appeared in the *Times* and drew considerable attention back in Massillon. "Weston Praises Cletus Wampler," trumpeted a front-page headline in Friday's *Evening Independent*. You can almost see Wampler's friends pounding him on the back with congratulations.

The midwestern roads were a respite—straighter and less meandering than many New York and Pennsylvania routes, enabling him to maintain a more consistent westerly direction. To the uninitiated, an easterner say, unfamiliar towns like Youngstown, Massillon, and Wooster might not have meant much. But to Weston, every town was critical, a conquest of sorts and another notch along the route. For all the tales of hardship detailed in Weston's daily dispatches, there was an equal number of testimonials about warm receptions and the kindness of strangers. It was compelling reading in the *Times*, so much so that the newspaper took to moving many of Weston's articles from the sports section to the news section, a sure sign that more people would see them. In the meantime, letters to the editor about Weston continued to flock in, like the one on

April 7 from Frank Parsons of New York, which suggested the paper turn the dispatches into a book. "As a daily reader of the exceedingly interesting letters from Edward Payson Weston . . . I write to suggest that steps be taken to preserve the communications in some more permanent form," Parsons urged. "I am sure they would appeal to a sufficient number of readers to make the understanding a paying one."

Readers soon got a jarring glimpse into one of Weston's more intense days. On Thursday, April 8, the weather gods were angry, showering Weston on his thirty-eight-mile jaunt to Mansfield with a storm of biblical proportions. It was a gale— the area's worst in a half-century, an old-timer told Weston. Onward through the day, the storm raged, hurling winds at seventy miles per hour "right into my teeth," the pedestrian added. That wind was of a ferocity that Weston had never before experienced, knocking him around the road like a punch-drunk fighter and twice under a fence. Stubbornly, the old walkist gutted it out, laboring forward and politely turning down requests from residents to join them in their homes until the storm blew through. For today at least, Weston wouldn't think of it, saying he "never had the least desire to slow down." Onward he walked for seven grueling hours before stopping just after noon in Ashford some twenty-four miles in.

The morning's effort would have tuckered out a pack of mules. Not Weston, who napped for a half hour and lunched before heading the final fourteen miles into Mansfield. As in Canton, he was anxious to get there in daylight to draw a bigger crowd. That in turn would help generate interest for his lecture the following evening. He got there, and indeed, the crowds came—some of whom had driven miles for a glimpse of the great man. Among them were the Mansfield police chief Jacob Weil and two cars full of the town's finest along with a dozen mounted policemen, who escorted the old pedestrian into the city. And it's a good job they did, because by the time

Weston had reached the Southern Hotel, where he would stay, some ten thousand people had turned out to give what he called a "most hearty welcome."

That was Weston's estimate, give or take a few thousand. It's a staggering figure given the population of Mansfield, which according to the 1910 census was a shade above twenty thousand. That meant one in every two residents greeted the pedestrian that day, a 1909 version of an astronaut or Elvis descending on Mansfield. Weston lapped it up, deciding to take a break from the routine and remain through Friday, for his lecture. Fortified by the extra R&R and with the cheers still ringing in his ears, Weston skipped about town Thursday with an extra bounce in his step. Even the weather was better—and with Mansfield still buzzing over the intensity of the winds, Weston joked to Mayor Huntington Brown that it must have been part of his effort to keep him out of town. Hardly. That afternoon, Weston addressed five hundred high school students; in the evening, he spoke at the YMCA.

Week four still had one day of substantial walking. It was Saturday's whopping fifty-three-mile trek to Toledo, where Weston planned to rest Sunday. Even with the rains, the gales, and all the snows of early spring in Ohio, Weston was game for anything short of a tsunami. The pedestrian trekked steadily and uneventfully most of the day, giving him a newfound appreciation for the basics. "This is the first real walking day I have had since I began this effort," Weston wrote after reaching Toledo. With the road in "elegant condition," he said, he didn't have to crisscross or follow the edge of the route because of mud or washouts. For Weston, a mudless day was a good day, a real luxury.

Also a luxury were all the company and best wishes of people he had met on his 1907 trek through the area. Stopping at the Fremont Hotel, he dined with the proprietors, Mr. and Mrs. Otis Davis, who two years before had nursed him back to health after the pedestrian had downed some rotten clams. Five miles southeast of Toledo, Weston pulled over at a farmhouse and napped for forty minutes, enabling him to enjoy a sensational reception as he, Police Chief Perry Knapp, and a squadron of patrolmen headed downtown to the Boody House hotel. Having covered just short of one thousand miles in twenty-three days of walking, Edward Payson Weston was set to enjoy a welcome day's rest.

7

"A Trifle Older Than I Was Twenty-Five Years Ago"

Sunlight streamed through the windows of Edward Payson Weston's hotel room on April 11, 1909, Easter Sunday. The radiance of this day of rest matched his mood: how remarkable, Weston thought, that the streets in Toledo had been thick with people Saturday to greet him, without a single policeman having to carry so much as a baton. So massive was the admiration for this seventy-year-old legend seeking to walk all the way to San Francisco.

That was apparent back in his hometown as well. The *New York Times* led its sports section that Sunday with the latest dispatch from the old pedestrian and a spread of three photos from his recent jaunt through upstate New York: a nifty portrait of Weston posing with several dozen residents of Randolph, a solitary shot of him in raingear headed down a dirt highway, and another of him dining in Corfu. The spread overwhelmed several other pieces in the day's paper, starting with a piece about France's Louis Orphee winning Saturday's Boston Marathon. Weston's walk also earned substantially better placement than the announcement that Henry Ford of the Ford Motor Company would enter two twenty-horsepower Model T cars as the only entrants of an ocean-to-ocean car race in June. The winner would receive the M. Robert Guggenheim Trophy, which

Ford was happy to support, predicting the race would "give Americans an opportunity to appreciate the vast possibilities of the motor car."

Guggenheim was a car buff, a twenty-four-year-old heir to the Guggenheim fortune whose New York–to–Seattle race was ostensibly to assist the "good roads" movement. But in reality, it was a celebration of speed at a time when people were paying close attention to how long it took to drive across the continent. A six-cylinder Franklin had set the record in fifteen days, two hours, and ten minutes in 1906—the same year a Buick set the standard for passenger cars, covering the distance from San Francisco to New York in twenty four days and eight hours. The Guggenheim drivers took considerably longer—twenty-three days in their car driven by Bert Scott to take the prize in Seattle and tell the tales of washed-out roads, muddy and snowy mountain passes, zealous policemen enforcing twenty-mile-per-hour speed limits, and spotty directions. At first Ford's Model T was declared the winner, which prompted a publicity campaign gushing that its winning vehicle was a "standard stock car and exact duplicate" of the kind available at local dealers. But that boast was quickly hushed five months later when the Ford was disqualified because of rule violations and the Shawmut was declared the winner. Years later a Ford mechanic admitted he wasn't looking when an overeager dealer may have changed the engine.

But both Guggenheim and Ford were on to something. The car revolution was in full force by 1909 with these gas-guzzling machines already starting to clog the roads. Just a decade before, in 1899, there were twenty-six car fatalities in the United States, but by 1909 the figure had jumped to 1,174, an alarming 53 percent per year. The numbers would continue to skyrocket, increasing nearly fourfold by 1914 and not falling for nearly two decades. You can guess what Weston thought: in the same spirit he disliked marathon running, he hated sharing the road with cars, and not just because of safety and congestion but because it discouraged exercise.

Production of the Model T dated to September 1908 and was already starting to revolutionize how people traveled. Ford's car was a revelation that was nicknamed the Tin Lizzy for its simple, homely appearance and design, which proved to be its major selling point. Designed to handle deep ruts and muddy roads, the Motel T appealed particularly to farmers in rural areas where, as Weston knew better than anyone, roads could be rutty and muddy. Equipped with an in-line four-cylinder engine, the car reached speeds up to thirty-five miles per hour and was available for under $900, a bargain even for its era.

All those new cars, however, had one important benefit for Weston and other pedestrians. With a majority of the American roads inadequate to handle all the heavy pounding of the traffic, government officials had kicked off a series of wholesale paving and road-building programs. In the interest of speeding mail service to rural areas, the U.S. Post Office Department and the Office of Road Inquiry in 1896 launched a modest national program to upgrade the postal roads to isolated rural areas. Two years later, Los Angeles County took a cue from the railroads and began spreading oil over its earthen roads to keep down the choking dust in what would become a blueprint for municipalities nationwide. And just as Weston was venturing west in 1909, government officials in Wayne County, Michigan, discovered they could effectively solidify the roads with a concoction made of brick, granite, wood block, and Portland cement surfaces. Later in the year, the county paved a stretch of Woodward Avenue near Detroit, which at nearly twenty feet wide and a mile long became the nation's longest cement road.

In 1905, road improvement took a quantum leap forward when President Roosevelt signed the Agriculture Appropriations Act, which created an Office of Public Roads and specified that its director be a "scientist and have charge of all scientific and technical work." The director, Logan Walker Page, was just the man for the job: a progressive like Roosevelt, he undertook an aggressive program of experimental highway construction in areas ranging from Jacksonville, Florida, to Macon County, Missouri, and Mount Weather, Virginia. It was a start, though there was still a long way to go. In 1904 the United States had 108,283 miles of gravel roads; 38,622 roads composed of various materials like stone, sand, or shell; and still a whopping 1,977,908 miles of dirt roads. That Weston had trekked the vast majority of his first nearly one thousand miles on those dirt roads during his great American trek of 1909—and had done so with spotty maps and without a car for the last ten days—only underscores the kinds of challenges he faced more than a century ago.

. . .

Stretching west from Toledo, the route looked favorable. So did the weather. After a rejuvenating Sunday, Weston faced a long sixty-two-mile trek to Bryan, close to the Indiana state line, and wanted to leave as early as possible on Monday. So on Sunday evening, the pedestrian took a nap, waking at 11:00 p.m. and sitting down forty minutes later to a substantial getaway supper at the Boody House. What wasn't to like?

The directions, that's what. Just after midnight, Weston was seen off at the city limits by six policemen and about two hundred townspeople as he began pushing west for Delta, some twenty-four miles along a road that today is Route 2. Dependent on faulty maps and his chauffeur for directions, Weston wandered off the road north and then west, saying later that several people had warned his driver that they were on the wrong road, though "he did not see fit to consult with me." Thinking he was headed the right way, Weston plunged ahead in the darkness, content that the roads, though on the sandy side, were still accessible.

Then things went completely to pieces. Twelve miles from Toledo, the car got stuck in the sand. Around 3:00 a.m. several residents informed Weston that he was lost, really lost, and nowhere near Delta. At least the locals, including a good-natured farmer, managed to send the old pedestrian back on track, but it wasn't before he had to tramp in and out of the woods and through a lot of ditches. Furious at his driver, the inaccurate maps, and the world in general, Weston cursed a blue streak. Things turned marginally better just after 5:00 a.m. when he was generously fortified with Mrs. J. N. Morrell's hot coffee and buttered bread, though he realized then that he had only made it to Swanton, which was halfway to Bryan. It meant Weston had tramped an extra twelve miles, all before dawn.

Weston would get to Delta by walking thirty-six miles—not the twenty-four he had expected. That was the least of his litany of errors on a bad day. Later Weston would say he had slept badly in Toledo and would never have set off early Monday if were it not for the big premidnight getaway feast. "A chapter of mistakes . . . I never should have tried to exceed this limit of stupidity," Weston said. "It is only when I do some foolish thing that I am made to realize that I am a trifle older than I was twenty-five years ago." Weston's anger at himself speaks of more than a simple temper tantrum: like many elite athletes, Weston, haunted by the threat of failure, was hardest on himself—content when things went well but never ever satisfied when things did not.

Problems piled up that miserable Monday. The maps failed again. Thinking the distance from Delta to the town of Archbold was twelve miles, Weston found it was seven more. Outside Wauseon, he took another wrong turn, adding more miles in the face of yet another gale, this one with winds of seventy-five miles per hour. Then, between Stryker and Bryan, the road turned into mushy, cakey clay, forcing Weston "to play checkers"—that is, walking forward at a kind of time-killing diagonal that kept at least some of the mud from sticking to his boots. Reaching Bryan, he was done and so exhausted that the cheers of spectators made him dizzy. The day's sole bright spot: the realization that he had now covered one thousand miles in twenty-nine days.

Tuesday, April 13, would be better. For starters, Weston decided to treat himself with a shorter day by ambling twenty-nine miles to Waterloo, less than half of Monday's distance. What a difference a day makes: pushing off in the early afternoon, Weston found roads packed with hard dirt, dry weather, and his aching left arm (aching from his fall the week before) much improved. "I am inclined to believe that the medical men are right when they say my recuperative powers are wonderful," Weston commented, "for that extra seven hours' rest put me once more on 'Easy Street.'"

"Easy" for him, that is. Planning to reach Chicago in two days, Weston had again become a marvel of endurance, hoping to implement what would become a maxim of distance runners by alternating "easy" days with longer, harder ones. So Wednesday's trek to Goshen, outside Elkhart, was a "hard" day of fifty-one miles, though you would never know it from Weston's renewed spirits. It was halfway through April, but the roads in northern Indiana were frosty when the old pedestrian had taken off at 5:00 a.m. that day. However the roads proved solid, "the best I've seen to date," and dotted with farmhouses filled with families ready with snacks and creating an old-fashioned Hoosier rolling welcome.

It was as if whole towns had turned out. In Kendallville and in Ligonier, where three hundred students had been dismissed from class for the occasion, there were crowds to greet him. Arriving in Goshen at *2:30 a.m.*, Weston was greeted by about fifty night owls who had waited up just to pass along their regards. Fortified by ever warmer temperatures and continued good roads, Weston appeared to be streaking across Indiana—forty-two miles on Thursday, April 15, through South Bend to New Carlisle, and another fifty-three on Friday, to Hobart, just south of Gary.

Spring had arrived. Back in New York on Thursday, April 15, thirty thousand spectators jammed the Polo Grounds to watch the Giants fall 3–0 in their home opener in thirteen innings to their crosstown rivals, the Brooklyn Superbas. At least New York's American Leaguers, the future Yankees, had a better day of it, opening on the road and besting the Washington Senators, 4–1, behind Jack Quinn's five-hit pitching. On Saturday Weston awoke for the relatively short twenty-one-mile jaunt into Chicago, but he again had car difficulties that tacked on extra mileage. This time, his driver had gone missing, leaving Weston with no one to chart the route through the twisting streets of Hammond. The locals helped where they could, but this latest driving mishap meant the pedestrian had to nearly double the distance of what should have been a ten-mile stretch.

Weston could barely wait to get to Chicago. Carl Sandburg's City of Big Shoulders was his kind of town, where he had ended several of his other big walks and had a legion of friends. Brash, brawling, and blue-collar, Chicago was about to throw another hearty welcome for this longest U.S. trip of Weston's career; this one would be bigger than the receptions of all those small Indiana hamlets put together. Greeting him at the city line were a protective gaggle of blue-coated policemen and an acquaintance, the former alderman of the Eleventh Ward and fellow walkist Joseph Badenoch, who in 1907 had trekked ninety miles from Milwaukee to Chicago in fifty-three hours. The contingent put in a full day's work by wending sixteen miles all the way to Weston's destination, the Illinois Athletic Club. Arriving at 6:30 p.m. Saturday, Weston would be wined, dined, and presented with a gold watch and fob, before resting on Sunday. Saturday's 40-mile walk had given him 276 for the week, the top weekly total to date. In the first twenty-seven days of his great walk across America, Weston had covered more than 1,200 miles—averaging 47 per day.

In Chicago Weston took stock. The Midwest promised flatter roads and a few rolling hills—and Weston could count on temperatures continuing to climb. Thinking and amending his projected western schedule, the pedestrian planned some modest changes. Looking to average forty-five miles a day, he decided that he needed more rest and would ease into each week by following his Sunday respite with a mild Monday of *only* thirty miles. Tinkering with his projected route, he decided that instead of heading due west across north-central Illinois toward Iowa, he would travel downstate in a south-southeast direction through Bloomington and Springfield, cross the Mississippi River into St. Louis, and *then* head west. It wasn't the most direct way, but Weston figured the amended route promised bigger towns and more opportunities to replenish his wallet by lecturing. He would come to regret not taking the more direct route.

In the meantime, Weston resolved to pack it in earlier on days when he was dragging. And with those unfortunate wanderings in the darkness of dawn outside Toledo still at the top of his mind, he resolved to forego the midnight starts, for now anyway, and stick to walking in daylight. He would be more flexible as well in the West, deciding to rest on the really scorching days during the hottest hours, especially between 11:00 a.m. and 3:00 p.m. With those details ironed down, there was one more bedeviling obstacle, one that Weston remained in Chicago through Monday, April 18, to sort out: securing a new support team. Weston's two trainers were long gone, and his driver soon would be as well. The old pedestrian had grown exasperated not so much by his car troubles in the mud but by the driver's erratic behavior, poor directions, and indifferent attitude. Enough was enough.

"It is absolutely necessary for me to have someone about me who can do something besides eat and sleep, and give a little attention," Weston said. So after sixty phone calls Monday and a lot of planning and talking with his supporters back in New York, Weston arrived at a partial solution—finding a valet but not yet a driver. He didn't fret; and relishing the additional day's rest, he resolved to start slowly Tuesday, April 20, with a forty-mile trek southwest to Joliet. In the meantime, five volunteers delivered his luggage down the road. And wouldn't you know it—twenty miles out of Chicago, the car stalled in the mud. Twenty miles later, a driverless Weston strolled into Joliet still in need of a car and an attendant. In effect, it was a sign, one that forced Weston to come to a final decision after all.

. . .

Even after his first great walk from Boston to Washington DC, Edward Payson Weston wasn't planning to be a professional pedestrian. Nor was he planning to after completing his second great walk, the one that took him from Washington DC back to Boston in 1862. That's because by then, Weston had become a wanted man.

Until then, walking had been his hobby, the kind of highly publicized lark practiced by someone who is twenty-two but probably not thirty-two. But so effective had Weston been in delivering the batch of mail to those Union troops in 1861 that the U.S. Army came calling again. So in 1862 or 1863 Weston joined the army, regularly delivering mail on foot from Boston and New York to soldiers in Washington DC and points south.

The job was more dangerous than it appeared. It required not just endurance but the ability of getting to Washington DC through Maryland, where Southern sympathies ran deep. The capital city was full of Confederate leanings, spies, and intrigue during the Civil War. President Lincoln himself could gaze from the second story of the White House just a few miles across the Potomac River and see a Confederate flag flying in Alexandria, Virginia, which was enemy territory. The distance to the Confederate capital, Richmond, was only 108 miles.

Was Weston a solider? Was he a spy? He may have been one or the other or both. Whatever he was, he flourished. Discovering his inner Shakespeare, Weston learned to conceal the mail while often pretending to be someone he wasn't. Finding a bridge guarded by Confederate sympathizers, he walked ten miles upstream before finding a boat to take him across the river, only to be stopped by a Southern farmer who insisted the baby-faced Weston was too young to be traveling alone. Perhaps out of paternalism or possibly suspicion, the farmer insisted Weston stay on the farm and go to work for him for a salary of twenty-five cents a month and board. Weston never said exactly how he escaped this sticky situation, but he did, presumably using his feet to get away.

At times, Weston's reputation preceded him. Working undercover, he once slipped into a friend's house in Media, Pennsylvania, just west of Philadelphia, for a few hours of sleep. His friend, however, was a blabbermouth and couldn't resist boasting to everyone in town about the visit of his famous friend, the great pedestrian. By the next morning, with a good chunk of Media's citizenry hoping to greet him, Weston made a quick exit out the back window.

From there, things only got dicier. Walking briskly to Washington, Weston knocked off seventy miles in less than twenty-four hours, only to be mistaken as a Confederate spy. Tossed into a Union guardhouse cell, he was interrogated for hours but managed to convince his captors that they were on the same side. The Union soldiers put him on a train to Annapolis, where the New York and Massachusetts regiments were stationed and got their mail from Weston.

Captured more than once by Confederates, Weston became adept at escaping certain execution by using his slight frame, boyish looks, and ability to mimic the regional dialect and pass for a local farm boy. He learned to avoid unfriendly dogs, who could raise a ruckus with their barking, and would admit later that "I was always afraid of dogs, especially at night." And back in New York he parlayed several flattering newspaper articles about his exploits into gifts from prestigious men's stores, who wished to clothe him for his undercover journeys. From Brooks Brothers came a disguise as a Susquehanna River boatman. The G. W. White Hat Company donated a hat. So went the world of the undercover agent, with several newspaper articles claiming outright that he was a spy and others not so sure. Only Weston knew for sure. "Being the flamboyant star-of-the-show type he was, [Weston] probably started the rumor himself," his great-granddaughter Joyce Litz wrote.

Weston never talked in detail about his war experience; but similar to many veterans, his service was among the seminal events of his life. How could serving during the most seismic era in American history not have a profound effect? Consider Weston's delight every time a veterans group paid their respects during his 1909 walk; those who served shared a special bond, the knowledge that they had been participants in something terrible and extraordinary, an experience they would never forget. "Probably that is why our old Civil War veterans in their final years seemed so clannish," wrote the great Civil War historian Bruce Catton, who traced his fascination with the era to the stories of the old vets he heard as a small boy growing up in early twentieth-century Michigan. "They stuck together as much as they could because they shared an understanding other folk did not have. Like Adam, they had been cast out of the enchanted garden, leaving innocence behind . . . The point to remember about these Civil War soldiers is that they came from a much less sophisticated age than any soldiers who have appeared since then. They had more innocence to lose, they had farther to fall."

After the Civil War, Weston went back to New York and resumed his position at the *Herald* as a messenger boy and then as a police reporter. Without telephones and with only horses to get about the clogged streets of New York, Weston used his fleet feet to give him an edge. He relished his ability to reach the scene of a news story on foot and then head back to the office to get his copy back to the editor, in some cases, before rival reporters were even on the scene.

Life for Weston was good, or so it seemed. At some point in the early 1860s, he married Maria Fox of Connecticut and lived north of New York in a home along the Hudson River, from which he walked into work every day because he said it was faster than taking the tram. By 1865 he and Maria had resettled in Medford, Massachusetts, where their first daughter, Lillian, was born. The family would have two other children: Maude, in 1867, and Ellsworth, in 1869.

But the Westons' marriage was not a happy one. Ed and Maria were polar opposites. Whereas he fancied himself as not just as a newspaperman and a pedestrian but a gambler and entrepreneur who would make and then lose a bundle, she was a genteel, conservative New Englander and "a creature of habit, who clung to her routine ways all her life," wrote his great-granddaughter, Joyce Litz. At home, Ed set the tone. Eccentric, outgoing, and restless, he did as he pleased and never recognized Maria's struggle for a more orderly life. Sometimes the family bank account was plentiful; other times it wasn't. Home life was unsettled and at best, "an anxiety-charged atmosphere," Litz wrote, in which Maria pinched pennies and held out hope for the riches that never materialized or for, at least, a steady income. Ed, in the meantime, squandered dollars, left the house duties to Maria, and kept his own schedule—staying up all night if he felt like it and sleeping all day when tired. Though

Weston claimed to believe in old-fashioned discipline, routine bored him. "Forever looking for change and excitement," Litz wrote, Weston "noisily condemned detail-oriented people."

By the winter of 1866 Weston was heavily in debt, telling the *Providence Journal* that he had lost everything and was subsisting on handouts from friends. "For months, I toiled to try and gain even a small amount to pay [them] on account, but could barely gain a living for my family," he wrote. "I am naturally ambitious, and happening to meet Mr. Goodwin at a time when I was very low spirited, he asked me if I could walk yet."

"Goodwin" was George K. Goodwin, who had risen from owner of a Boston pawnshop to a major New York circus and theater entrepreneur and manager of the humorist Artemus Ward. In Weston, Goodwin saw a gamble worth taking; and in the summer of 1867 he placed a sizable bet that Weston could walk from Portland, Maine, to Chicago, some 1,226 miles, in thirty days. Make it under the deadline and the pedestrian would earn $10,000. Weston would have to get use to the Post Road and at some point cover one hundred miles in a twenty-four-hour period, getting five attempts to do so. Fail and he would have to forfeit $6,000 of his stake.

Some criticized his decision to turn professional, his family included. They considered it a crass, low-class way to make a living and hardly something a responsible gentleman would do. "His respectable relatives didn't understand him," his daughter Lillian Weston wrote in a 1924 magazine profile of her father. "They regretted he did not embrace a dignified occupation like banking, or selling groceries, insurance or dry goods." Lillian was an exception and would grow to appreciate her father, even though he wasn't there much during her upbringing. "They never accepted him as the great athlete he was," she wrote. "To make a man with my father's erratic disposition lead a humdrum life would be like hitching a race horse to a plow."

Preparing in 1867 to walk to Chicago, Weston fired back at his critics, particularly those who compared pedestrianism to what many considered the ruffian sport of prizefighting. "They think because my Maker has endowed me with perhaps greater walking abilities than most of my fellow men, and because I walk for a wager, no matter to what laudable purpose my winnings will be applied, if I am successful, that I must be classed with prize fighters [*sic*]," he wrote to the *Providence Journal*. "Now this is a slander of an honest man who is willing to do anything under the sun that will legitimately enable him to liquidate his debts."

Weston said he had never even been to a prizefight. He called himself "a plain business man" who failed to see what he was doing wrong. "If baseball or boat racing is a crime then I am wrong," he wrote. "Otherwise, I am right." Feeling justified, Weston on Tuesday, October 29, 1867, kicked off his first great professional trek, barreling up Federal Street in Portland en route to Chicago.

Once again, there were crowds. Those who followed could only keep up for a few blocks. In Boston, thousands turned out to applaud Weston as he repeatedly lifted his white Marseilles hat to the multitudes. Stopping at the Parker House Hotel, he made a brief appearance on the balcony just so everyone could get a look.

Deciding to incorporate several changes, Weston donned natty new attire. This time he dressed in a dark-blue cloth jacket and trousers to match, red woolen stockings, and heavy boots laced to the ankles. Matched with that sleek white hat topped with a button, he resembled a stylish gentleman out for a Sunday stroll, a very lengthy stroll. This time, he carried not a cane but a switch, which he was obliged to use vigorously over the heads and shoulders of enthused admirers who impeded his progress. And this time, he didn't stock booklets extolling the glories of Grover and Baker sewing machines but thirty thousand copies of blatant self-promotion—his own little newsletter. Called *The Time Table*, it included his tentative walking schedule and a photo of himself and cost twenty-five cents.

History doesn't record how many newsletters Weston sold on the walk. No question it was a lot, putting him in the company of growing legions of politicians, actors, and other public figures who had taken to mass distributing their images for promotion. Everyone, it seemed, was looking to give away their likeness ever since the day less than two decades ago when an Englishman named Frederick Scott-Archer had invented the "wet collodion plate." This new process produced unlimited images from a negative—a vast improvement over the previous technology that limited each exposure to a single daguerreotype. Running for president in 1860, a savvy Abraham Lincoln took advantage of the power of this new and cheap technology to familiarize voters with what he looked like. So did a certain actor–turned–presidential assassin named John Wilkes Booth, whose cold, penetrating eyes would soon stare from his daguerreotype photos, which would find a place on the famous "Wanted" posters from April 1865.

Using a switch to beat back a crowd sounds beastly, but it was needed for Weston. The crowds could be fanatical. Making his first pass at covering one hundred miles in twenty-four hours between Dedham, Massachusetts, and Andover, Connecticut, Weston was thrown to the ground by a surging horde in Pawtucket, Rhode Island, and nearly dislocated his left hip. The pedestrian was okay; but after a couple of hours later in Providence, he was escorted by a fleet of policemen in what soon became a normal safety measure.

But Weston was indebted to all the people, even the unruly ones, who came out to watch him on his great walk of 1867. In a nation of avid newspaper readers and small towns, where everyone knew everyone else's business, it was easy to follow the great walkist's path. He was colorful and provided a great interview, which the papers exploited. His decision to walk halfway across a country just two years beyond the devastation of a Civil War far worse than anyone could ever have predicted was one of the first feel-good stories in years. Easy to root for—or against, in the case of some gamblers—Weston was a tonic for the shattered families still reeling from a war of appalling devastation: some 625,000 casualties and 412,000 wounded in a nation of 29 million. Could a man going for a walk make a difference? In a nation with plenty of widows, orphans, and men still shattered from their experience or too disabled to tend the crops or look for work, the answer was a definitive "yes." Two years after Appomattox, Weston's walk was a pleasant diversion, a small source of renewal for a country that needed to smile.

Weston's first attempt to walk one hundred miles in twenty-four hours created a storm of attention. At Providence, his home town, he was thirty-two miles into his "century" and eighteen minutes ahead of his projected timetable as crowds cheered his every step, handed him wreaths, and serenaded him through their towns. But in the desolate early morning darkness of the sandy and rough roads, Weston's hip got sore, forcing him to abandon the attempt. A snowstorm outside Great Barrington, Massachusetts, took care of attempt number two. Trying again in Silver Lake, Ohio, just north of Akron, he pulled up into Conneaut with badly swollen feet and unable to take another step, just nine miles short of his objective. To ease the pain throughout the day, Weston had poured liberal amounts of whiskey on his feet, but it hadn't been enough to stop the pain.

The walk and his difficulty in achieving the century was big news. Most everyone, save some gamblers, admired Weston and rooted for him. At Erie, Pennsylvania, the crowds who gathered were so spirited that a police escort used subterfuge, sending him through a side door of the National Hotel. Most recognized the immense hardships posed by weather extremes, poor roads, darkness, and unimpressed dogs in walking one hundred miles in twenty-four hours.

Weston still had his critics. Some correspondents suggested that Weston could easily have made the century and was holding back as part of a betting ring, which the *Cleveland Herald* wrote had turned him into "a stool pigeon by the men who have him under control." The paper never revealed the names of the men involved but reported the tale of a man who it said had raked in $80,000 to $100,000 by betting against the pedestrian. "Weston has no trainer; never had a trainer; does not require a trainer," the *Cleveland Herald* correspondent wrote. "I have not the slightest doubt that he can make the 100 miles in 24 hours whenever he chooses to do so or whenever his owners choose that he shall do so. . . . The apprehension of danger manifested by Weston, in all of his movements arises from the fact that persons who are not in the 'ring,' may attempt private personal injury—perhaps death—in order to win large sums of money against him." Still, everyone agreed that Weston's decision to peddle photographs of himself was paying off handsomely; by the time he reached Buffalo, the pedestrian was reported to have already netted $15,000 from the photos.

For every detractor, Weston drew a thousand times as many staunch supporters. Trekking through Ohio, the great mid-nineteenth-century American clown and entertainer Dan Rice greeted Weston in the middle of a wind storm so intense that Rice figured his carriage would blow over. "Clouds of dust and gravel were flying in our faces, compelling the driver to stop a number of times, as both he and the horses were completely blinded," Rice wrote. "Nor was it a temporary commotion of the elements, for almost a hurricane kept full possession of the night. . . . I did not deem it possible for him to proceed. Judge, then, of my astonishment when I learned the next morning that he had successfully battled through that long tempestuous night and was untiringly striding on to apparent victory."

Rice was referring to reports that the ninety-one miles Weston had covered between Silver Creek and Conneaut was in fact, a century. The *Cleveland Plain Dealer* claimed to have measured the distance by stage road, which it put at *101* miles. Even so, Weston vowed to try again to walk one hundred miles in twenty-four hours, this time in Indiana. Again, he got close but not close enough—tramping eighty-six miles over uneven, rain-soaked roads, across streams, and past surging crowds. Some fourteen miles short and less than three hours to reach his goal of New Castle, an exhausted Weston threw in the towel. An admirer had stepped on his ankle, making it sore, and the pedestrian was discouraged. "I can't do it and I'll be damned if I am going to kill myself in this effort," he snapped to reporters.

So Weston wouldn't try again to reach the century mark on his great journey to Chicago, though he may have accomplished the feat back in Ohio. That he had failed—or possibly made it after all—fed his legend. Most everybody walked, especially in the mid-nineteenth century, so who couldn't relate to him? Weston didn't always succeed but tried mightily hard to do so—and in the process, he generated a lot of excitement. That was magnified when people were lucky enough to be on his route and watch him walk by, or even walk a ways with him. Weston was a national sportsman with the soul of a great Shakespearean actor. "It was the theater's loss when Edward Payson Weston became a pedestrian rather than an actor," the Broadway actor E. A. Southern once said of him. A case in point came a day beyond his last century attempt, outside LaPorte, Indiana, where an elderly woman led a beautiful younger woman to meet him. Placing the young woman's hand in his hand, the elderly woman told Weston that the young woman was blind and had taken a great interest in his welfare. Moved nearly to tears, he would never forget the moment. Nothing, he said, had ever touched him more deeply.

Gregarious by nature and comfortable in the limelight—fortunate character traits for a solitary profession—Weston was unfailingly sincere and, at heart, an optimist. That is why every good meal was the "best" meal he had ever had, and the most recent cup of coffee, the absolute most fantastic he had ever enjoyed. At the time, he meant it; and with the exception of occasional tantrums, like the one outside New Castle, he was almost always exceptionally gracious. Nor did it hurt that shortly before leaving on this particular trip, Weston made the vow to his mother to never walk on the Lord's Day, a pledge he stuck to till death.

Apparently, Weston's mother, Marie, was dead set against her only son making the long trip, arguing that the unusual hours would trigger an unsavory lifestyle, turning him into a drunkard and a gambler. Weston, along with several of his sisters, begged that she change her mind, saying it would be the "making of him." Marie would eventually grant her blessing but only on the condition that Weston never, ever walk between midnight Saturday and midnight Sunday. At times, Weston was sorely tempted to change his mind, such as in Paris years later when he was alone and nearly broke and promised $5,000 for an eight-day walking demonstration that included two Sundays and was so easy it was like "falling off a log." Down to his last few sous, Weston didn't break his pledge, a decision he never regretted even after receiving a letter from a sister a short time later informing him their mother had died.

Among all those residents of small towns for whom Weston was a role model, who couldn't relate?

. . .

Nearing the end of his great 1867 trek to Chicago, Edward Payson Weston was the man of the hour. It was Tuesday, November 28, and from early in the morning, streams of people headed into the city from all directions to see the great pedestrian close out his triumphant journey. Approaching from the southeast, Weston was met at Twenty-Second Street by the thirty-piece Great Western Light Guard Band, which launched, appropriately, into tunes ranging from "See the Conquering Hero Comes" to "The Arkansas Traveler." The band had a further purpose: shielding Weston as he briskly trudged along, smiling broadly and waving his elegant white hat. Estimates of the crowd ran to as many as fifty thousand, not that anyone had a precise figure or cared. "Make your own estimates of the numbers upon this basis, a solid mass of humanity, one hundred feet wide [and] three miles long, and you can guess the number as well as we," reported the *Chicago Journal*.

That was accurate. Only two years removed from the end of the Civil War, the crush of happy humanity gathered to simply watch a man just walk by was unprecedented. Headed downtown, Weston turned onto Monroe Street and, from Madison, went up Dearborn Street, then Lake and Clark to Sherman Street, where he would lead the procession like a stage manager around the courthouse all the way to the Sherman House Hotel. There he ventured to the balcony and, like royalty or at least a political candidate, addressed the multitudes.

Weston rose to the occasion. Impulsively scooping up the hotel owner's curly haired two-year-old daughter, he waved his hat with gusto and, with an actor's timing, obliged the multitudes ever so briefly. "Gentlemen, I have a short speech to make, but it is for the little one here," he said. "I have now won the pony for this baby!" That was it, and the cheers rang out. Pecking his new friend on her forehead, he waved again and ducked inside the hotel. "Not Grant nor Sherman, nor any of our country's heroes, were ever made the subject of more ardent curiosity on the part of our citizens than the hero of the 1,000-mile walk," the *Chicago Tribune* wrote. "The excitement at times reached almost to the point of frenzy and in their eagerness to gain a standing point right in front of the window at which the beaming man was seen, the crowd came in sharp collision with the police."

Weston wasn't staying at the Sherman House. His quarters were at the Opera House, where he and his handlers retired to talk strategy and to try to profit from the attention. Though it's difficult to say precisely when Weston decided to become a professional pedestrian for good, he may have decided once and for all in the afterglow of this triumphant walk west. Still fired up, Weston turned his sights to Great Britain, where walking was big. "If any Englishman undertakes to beat what I have done," he boasted, "then I will go to England and lick the hell out of them."

But Weston wasn't finished in Chicago. He decided to give several public lectures—charging $1.50 admission for afternoon and evening talks at the Opera House. By doing so, he became part of a real American tradition, a mid-nineteenth-century explosion of traveling lecturers focused on a self-educating American populace hungry for knowledge. Many of the most famous speakers of the age had gotten their start in the antislavery movement of the 1850s; but for every William Lloyd Garrison, Susan B. Anthony, and Frederick Douglass, there were boatloads of politicians, prairie preachers, showmen, temperance advocates, and faith healers looking for a good night's pay on the speaking circuit. The lecturing wasn't restricted to any particular part of the country, with lonely miners and farmers in the Midwest and West often the most eager for a few hours of self-enlightenment and entertainment—and sometimes advice for curbing their drinking and gambling. It's no accident that the Chautauqua Institution, originally the Chautauqua Lake Sunday School Association, was founded just seven years later in southwestern New York.

Weston's Opera House lectures were a smash, earning the pedestrian some extra income. Reporters said later he cleared a total of $4,000 during his walk west, though it's not clear just how much he earned by talking about it. The lectures gave Chicagoans a chance not just to see the man of the hour but to glean the secrets of his success. Lecturing was Weston's effort to build his brand—an opportunity for insight into his private reasons for walking, his tactics, and health—and also to defend himself. "People argue that because I failed in my one-hundred-mile walk and yet walked seventy-two miles the next day that I might have [made the century] if I liked," he told the afternoon crowd. "I should have been very happy to have 'liked' to have done it if I could."

Weston spoke for only ten minutes, but packed a punch. Getting right to the point, he said he walked to relieve his family from "pecuniary embarrassment." For all the rousing success of his performance, his failure to officially reach the century in twenty-four hours nagged at him. "It is possible that if I had been wholly successful in it as I had tried, most earnestly tried, it might have been better for me," he said. "There is a time when every man must experience complete exhaustion. . . . He will go as far as he can, and go no further. . . . But when he recovers from exhaustion, he is not injured at all, but he can get up and do the same thing the following day."

For an untrained speaker, Weston was a revelation. Candid and self-deprecating, he was forthright and infused with devilish comic timing. All that time on the roads had made him a thinking man with considerable insight into what he did and why. Men relished his tales of the road. Women were said to admire his more philosophical insights. Clearly, he had a future in this side of the business, and his lectures in Chicago were dress rehearsals, a blueprint of sorts to the kinds of topics he would cover in a long career of public speaking. Professing to be no lecturer—"I [did] not know until today that I have ever made a speech before in my life, except once when I said, 'Not guilty,'"—Weston vowed to do the best he could.

So he did. "Walking as an exercise is something I wish to

see encouraged, something that I think will benefit the youth of America," Weston said. "It is . . . not only healthy, but it is a pleasure at times and as good an exercise as a man can take." To those who had criticized professional pedestrianism as a gutter sport along the lines of prizefighting, Weston offered a measured response. "There are many sports termed athletic sports such as gymnastics, rowing, yachting, baseball playing, horse racing, and pedestrianism," he said. "There are other sports termed brutal . . . such as dogfighting, cockfighting, and prizefighting. I have been associated [with] . . . prizefighters, [but] I say it here, as I have always said it, if it were for no other reason, if I had no principal to guide me [other] than the respect that I have for my mother, I would not allow myself to be associated with men who stand up and hammer each other's faces to pieces for a few thousand dollars."

To underscore his point, Weston related the story of his conversation with the minister before starting the walk to Chicago. "Weston, I think you can walk some, and the only bad feature about this is that you are walking on water," the man of God told him. "If you win the race you win quite a bit of money, and you are encouraging gambling."

"With due respect to the clergymen of America," the pedestrian replied, "I think if you should offer any [of them] $5,000 to walk from Portland, Maine, to Chicago, Illinois, in thirty consecutive days and he could do it, I think that he would be very apt to do it, and he would not contribute $2,500 of it to the American Tract Society. He didn't say that he would."

The audience roared. Delving into the background of his diet, Weston said that he used to eat moderately—buttered bread and a cup of coffee for breakfast and two other meals—but that walking long distances day after day required continual replenishment and an attitude adjustment. For Weston, that meant five or six hearty meals a day—so hearty and rich that a hotel-proprietor friend had suggested Weston "take pedestrian trips all [his] lifetime." That way, the proprietor would only have to board Weston for a week, rather than a month.

Tramping through New York, Weston was told by a hotel landlady that he was eating too much. "Mr. Weston," the proprietress told him at breakfast, "I take a motherly interest in you."

"I am very glad of it," Mr. Weston replied. "I like to have anyone to take a motherly interest in me. . . . And I asked her why."

"You will excuse my remarking that you are eating too much, and I don't think you had better have another egg," she said. "I should just as leave you would have it, but eggs will make you bilious!"

"I told her I should like to be bilious," Weston noted, "and therefore would take two eggs."

The crowd shook with laughter. Weston had won them over. In doing so, he had morphed from a curiosity to a crossover star, an athlete and a folk hero rolled into one. On December 4 at Farwell Hall, Chicagoans threw a benefit for Weston in which he lectured and demonstrated his four-, five-, and six-mile gaits as he lapped the auditorium. Some months later, he earned $1,000 for lecturing at Mercantile Library in St. Louis. Then Weston followed up by lapping the hall—*19 times*.

Any temptation Weston may have had to resume his previous preprofessional pedestrian days was done. By 1868 the legend had become a walker for life.

8

"Walking Is the Easiest Part"

A day's walk south of Chicago, Edward Payson Weston described himself as looking like "a drowned rat." Leaving Joliet in the driving rain of the predawn darkness of Wednesday, April 21, 1909, Payson had donned his oilskin coat, which didn't seem to do much good. And there was mud—and not just mud, but a deep, black form of goop that covered the entire roadway, "so slippery one could scarcely keep his feet," as Weston put it. Arriving just past 11:00 a.m. twenty miles down the road in Wilmington, with another twenty-one miles to go to reach his day's goal of Dwight, he was drenched to the bone and dirty as a miner.

So Weston stopped, changed, and pressed on. Continuing south, the roads got worse, flooding into pools of water. "I thought this was a task for walking," the pedestrian lamented, "but it seemed likely to develop into a swimming bout." So Weston bounded off the road and set off through the adjoining fields, fighting the whole way to keep the water from sweeping over his ankles. That worked until it didn't, giving Weston little option but to go back to the drenched road and continue walking.

The day had turned into a full-scale calamity of misfortunes. Though Weston had finally secured another car, it was a loaner and he would need to secure a permanent one to use in the West. In the meantime, he was finding his new attendant as hopeless as the last; arriving soaked in Wilmington, the old pedestrian was directed a mile beyond his destination hotel, because the new attendant had failed to scout a shorter route off the main road. And what of those two new hats that a friend had sent Weston from New York? Lost. Both of them. "I tell you right now," Weston said, "the walking is the easiest part of this task."

At least, the last part of the day was easier. Stopping to change in tiny Coal City, the pedestrian was greeted by five hundred residents and the town's Marine Band, many of whom escorted him to the city limits. The reception revived Weston—"I kept the crowd in the rear on a laughable and uproarious run," he boasted—and so did the roads. Stone ballasted and drier, those roads sustained Weston those last miles into Dwight.

. . .

The week was growing short. On Thursday, April 22, Weston remained in Dwight, home of the well-known Keeley Institute for treating alcoholism. His latest valet had quit after three days—imagine the tongue lashing *he* got—and the pedestrian still needed to find a reliable way once and for all to move his supplies. Stuck on the phone throughout the day, again, Weston and his backers made several crucial decisions. First, they ditched the car. Good riddance, too; it was more trouble than it was worth. Weston could do without it after all, given his decision to stick mostly to the railroad beds the rest of the way. Next, they chose a new manager who would follow Weston by riding the train—hurling him sacks of mail, food, and supplies as he could while trying to stay slightly ahead of the pedestrian in order to find accommodations. It wouldn't be perfect; for the first time in his long career, Weston would be pretty much on his own most days, joined by his manager as many evenings as possible. The walker and manager would have to work hard at keeping in touch—oh, how handy an iPhone would have been!—but Weston's uncommon touch at making friends with railroad officials and workers willing to help him would be a major advantage. So just like that, a sizable chunk of the trip's logistical challenges had cleared up. One day, Weston had been wound up about it, wondering how he could possibly make it all the way to San Francisco without the proper support team; and then in a day, it was solved. The walkist would barely again mention the issue.

So stepping off the train in Chicago and into Weston's life was his newest manager, one John C. Schinkel of New York. A bespectacled, square-jawed man in his early forties and a baker by trade, Schinkel looked sharp—dressing in a suit, vest, and a tie, topped off by a porkpie hat—and he would be a godsend with just the right amount of support, friendship, advanced planning, press relations, and the occasional coddling Weston required. It's almost certain that Schinkel was related to Weston's close friend Adolph Schinkel, the baker who was supplying Weston with homemade bread throughout the great trek.

Weston would periodically reference his "manager" in his dispatches, but never by name. How Schinkel was chosen and dispatched to Illinois was certainly the decision of Weston's New York backers, whom the walker also never named, referring to them as his "three musketeers" or "mascots." So who *were* they? Weston said only that they were Wall Streeters, two with addresses at 60 Wall Street and the other, Walter Moler, from 111 Broadway. They were financiers, and most likely fellow veterans, who supplied their pedestrian friend with periodic checks, telegrams of encouragement, and John Schinkel. Nor did Weston ever cite the specific amounts of the checks, though he gushed with heartfelt thanks at the arrival of each and every musketeerial telegram.

With Schinkel on board, Weston's confidence soared. So

FIG. 1. Weston the Rock Star: In 1867 Weston walked from Portland, Maine, to Chicago, covering more than 1,200 miles in twenty-six days and earning a $10,000 prize. Author's Collection.

FIG. 2. Fit as a Fiddle: Weston, looking confident, in a 1909 portrait. Prints & Photographs Division, Library of Congress LC-USZ62-74752.

FIG. 3. (*Opposite top*) Out for a Stroll: Weston (right) walks with a friend, Humphrey O'Sullivan, in early 1908. O'Sullivan was a self-made man from Lowell, Massachusetts, and a former print shop employee who patented the rubber heel for shoes. Prints & Photographs Division, Library of Congress LC-USZ62-74753.

FIG. 4. (*Opposite bottom*) Edward Payson Weston Trading Card. Weston was featured in this 1908 series by Mecca Cigarettes, "Series of Champion Athletes." Author's Collection.

FIG. 5. (*Above*) Face of a Pedestrian: Weston in an undated photo. George Grantham Bain Collection, Prints & Photographs Division, Library of Congress, LC-DIG-ggbain-08001.

FIG. 6. And He's Off: Weston sets off for Minneapolis on June 2, 1913, from the Plaza at the City College of New York. George Grantham Bain Collection, Prints & Photographs Division, Library of Congress, LC-DIG-ggbain-13119.

FIG. 7. How Do You Do?: Weston in an undated photo. George Grantham Bain Collection, Prints & Photographs Division, Library of Congress, LC-DIG-ggbain-07949.

EDWARD PAYSON WESTON

Fig. 8. A Break and a Photo: This
photograph of Weston during the
1909 walk was sold as a postcard.
Author's Collection.

did his enthusiasm, which practically bled through the pages of his dispatches from central Illinois. On Friday, April 23, Weston rose in the darkness, had a hearty meal, and feeling fit, left Dwight for Bloomington, fifty-four miles away. With his managerial troubles behind him, the pedestrian got right to his new strategy, following the Chicago and Alton Railway tracks, which promised a more direct, solid route as well. Even the weather was cooperating—it was clear and sunny—as were the maps. For the first time in a long while, Weston said, "the miles walked equaled the schedule." Reaching Pontiac in mid-morning, some eleven miles down the road, Weston was greeted by a cheering crowd, which boosted his spirits.

There were gracious thank-yous directed all around in Pontiac. But stop? Weston did briefly, but only to chug a cup of eggnog. With the weather and the roads cooperating, he was anxious to make up some of the time he had lost due to "valetgate." But in getting to Bloomington in time for his evening lecture at the YMCA, he caught a chill, which by Saturday had become a full-blown cold and backache during a thirty-mile trek to Lincoln. Chalk up another good deed to a stranger, in this case J. D. Douglas of the microscopic town of Shirley, just south of Bloomington, who on Saturday morning offered the old pedestrian a homemade meal and a bed. The resulting four-hour rest and sustenance worked wonders; feeling much refreshed, Weston bounded later that Saturday all the way to Lincoln.

The shorter distance was by design, part of Weston's new resolution to take things a tad easier when he wasn't feeling his best. The timing helped as well—Sunday, April 25, was a rest day, spent in part by assuring supporters back home that he was feeling better than ever, having recovered much of his old strength. "Through all my trip, the circumstances that combined last week to hold me back were the most annoying and the hardest to overcome," said Weston. "I am entirely refreshed and feel restored to normal condition after a night's rest, and I shall take the road Monday morning as fresh and strong as when I started from New York."

Weston's appetite was voracious, a good barometer of his level of fitness and health. His valet troubles were over. And despite all the flooding and mud, the weather was steadily getting more temperate, and the roads, drier and more level. "I have not seen anything resembling a hill for more than one hundred miles," the pedestrian boasted, exaggerating only slightly. Looking to take advantage of these positive circumstances, Weston kicked off week seven extra early—just after midnight Monday with hopes of covering a whopping fifty-five miles through Springfield, Illinois, to Girard, Missouri. It was the thirty-seventh walk day, and Weston felt strong from the get-go, breakfasting at 5:30 a.m. in Williamsville, seventeen miles down the road, and reaching Springfield, another thirteen miles south-southwest, just after 9:00 a.m. Napping for several hours in the early afternoon, the old pedestrian reached Auburn after 5:00 p.m. and Girard by 8:20 p.m. The day's only glitch was falling over a switched wire close to the end of the day's walk.

But on Tuesday Weston awoke, bathed, and felt no ill effects from the previous evening's fall. Feeling stronger with each day, he set out on the forty-nine-mile trek to Alton, Illinois, across the Mississippi River from St. Louis, along country roads he found better than ever; so much so that he lamented his decision, at least for the moment, to follow the railroads. One reason for his concern was that the railroad beds were on the outskirts of most towns, restricting the crowds. And walking along the ties was hard on his feet and slowed him to an average of three and a half miles per hour, one full mile per hour under his usual brisk pace. But the change to railroad walking would do for now, especially with the old pedestrian only now finding the strength and rhythm that had eluded him for weeks. And the crowds were still finding him, as they did in Carlinville, where students from Blackburn College hiked two miles north to meet and escort the old pedestrian the last two miles into Alton. There, more people applauded, and reporters from the St. Louis papers peppered him with questions, a reminder that he was nearing what would be his last big-city stop for quite a while.

Years later, a reporter who had walked with Weston during the last few miles of his journey into Alton recalled the twin challenge of keeping up with the seventy-year-old pedestrian while having to ask questions and scribble down his answers. He also remembered how one of the more prominent Blackburn College students ambling out to the road to walk those couple of miles into town was a football player "and a stout husky young man" who quickly discovered he could barely keep with the seventy-year-old pedestrian. Weston arrived invigorated, but the football player didn't. He had given up, exhausted by trying to keep pace.

Like a finely tuned Swiss clock, Weston just kept going, fortified by his otherworldly ability to recover quickly. That next day, Wednesday, April 28, he trekked another thirty-two miles to his quarters at the Missouri Athletic Club in St. Louis, a city where he had some history. Back in 1871—thirty-eight years earlier—the old pedestrian had walked two hundred miles there—*backward*. It was drizzling that Wednesday morning when Weston left Alton, heading south on the Illinois side of the Mississippi River and intending to cross into the city at East St. Louis. By the time he reached the little town of Brooklyn, Illinois, the sun was shining and he had attracted the usual gaggle of admirers.

How unfortunate that a policeman misread the hubbub and wasn't reading the newspapers. Brooklyn, also known as Lovejoy, wasn't just another town but America's first incorporated African American settlement. Established in the early nineteenth century as a town of free and enslaved African Americans who had escaped slavery, Brooklyn circa 1909 had grown to a settlement of black craftspeople, merchants, farmers, and laborers—and it was a national symbol of pride for African Americans. While the phenomenon of a seventy-year-old man tramping briskly through the center of town trailed by a group of enthused locals could be an odd site for the uninformed, it was an everyday occurrence for Weston, particularly in and around big cities.

Chances are the Brooklyn policeman hadn't been reading the newspapers filled with stories of Weston's impending appearance in St. Louis. Eyeing the stranger walking through town trailed by a crowd, the policeman cast a suspicious gaze on the pedestrian and approached him with a question.

"How do I know but what you may be is an escaped lunatic?" he asked Weston.

The pedestrian considered the question and conceded it wasn't completely off base. "He said that when a stranger walks through town with such a crowd following him, he had a right to have his suspicions aroused," Weston said of the policeman. "This was a funny incident, especially when my identity was made known."

The policeman had made an error in judgment. But he didn't apologize and walked away without another word.

On the surface, the incident was minor, a simple case of mistaken identity and poor manners. Within minutes, Weston was in East St. Louis, where he was greeted by an enthusiastic crowd before crossing the big river into St. Louis. But the pedestrian didn't forget and chose to mention the encounter in his daily write-up, which the *New York Times* turned into a storm, leading with the headline "Weston Arrested by Negro Officer." That may have been written by a copy editor in a hurry; Weston hadn't been arrested, just questioned, though he said in the article that he had been "detained," which probably meant he had merely been stopped and questioned. Though the pedestrian had mentioned the officer was black, the headline turned a minor misunderstanding into a racial incident with the underlying implication that the policeman was more than just inept, but black and inept.

A *Times* editorial on Friday, April 30, about the conduct of the "zealous negro policeman" and his suspicions of lunacy underscored the era's institutional racism. "For the great majority of [people] to attempt such a journey would certainly be madness," the paper wrote. "Weston, however, is different. In the first place, he likes walking, and the rest of us, or most of us, hate it except in carefully restricted quantities—and when there isn't a chance to ride. In the next place, he is capable of doing it without injury, or, at any rate, he always has been, and apparently has not changed, and, lastly, it is his business. So the negro policeman and others of like views may be reassured. Weston is . . . no measurable danger."

. . .

By ambling across the Eads Bridge at East St. Louis, Edward Payson Weston was doing more than just crossing the Mississippi River into St. Louis. He had arrived in Missouri, the true breadbasket of America and the sixth of the twelve states he planned to pass through on his epic walk to the Pacific. Until now, he had wandered mostly west but south and north as well. But from here on, the pedestrian's route would be a lot more direct—due west and a tad straighter as he followed a route parallel to today's Route 70. And for now at least, he had left the train routes for the more solid wagon roads.

Weston called the roads west from St. Louis, "the best I had ever walked over." He was following the old Santa Fe and Oregon Trails, more commonly known as Boonslick Road, which had formed in the mid-eighteenth century from the remnants of an Indian-trapper pathway in downtown St. Louis, becoming one of the first major western roads. Historians credit its curious name to the efforts by frontiersman Daniel Boone and his sons to extend the early trail to salt springs, or an animal "licking" place, in Saline County.

The route was a fresh phase in the trip, a renewal of sorts. To emphasize that point, Weston arrived on his fortieth day of walking just before noon on Thursday, April 29, in St. Charles, some twenty-three winding miles out of St. Louis, and got a physical. Dr. U. S. Grant Arnold's examination was positive, finding that Weston had both a good pulse and heart. That was fortunate, because between St. Charles and his destination for the day, twenty miles up the road in Wright City, Weston's path turned treacherous when four miles east of Wright City, near Wentzville, the skies turned black with clouds and delivered a torrent of hail, hard rain, and gale-force winds. Caught by the sudden violence of the storm, Weston sought shelter, which took some convincing of a suspicious farmer. Like the policeman from Brooklyn, Illinois, the farmer didn't recognize the great pedestrian. But at least he came around and helped Weston get out of the storm for a spell. All in all, it had been another good day, at the end of which Weston was forty-three miles closer to San Francisco.

It had turned cold. And the winds kept howling, fortified by the pancake flatness of the Missouri plains, which offered few opportunities of escape. So rising in the dawn of Friday, April 30, the old pedestrian decided to cut it short, at least by his standards. He targeted the hamlet of Montgomery City, forty-one miles away, and was able to get there, thanks again, to the kindness of strangers. Near Truesdale, one E. O. Kelly, station agent of the Wabash Railroad, recognized the old pedestrian and treated him at home to milk and bread. In Warrenton, cheering students from Central Wesleyan College helped Weston's spirits enough to will him through the last eleven miles to R. B. Cope's hotel in Montgomery.

Weather extremes would bedevil Weston's jaunt through Missouri. Approaching Montgomery, he confronted seventy-mile-per-hour winds. The biting cold grew worse the next day, Saturday, May 1, on the twenty-six-mile trek to Mexico, Missouri. Two days later, while crossing the Missouri River at Glasgow, Weston faced little choice beyond either walking miles out of his way or crossing a mile-long railroad trestle—while praying no trains were headed his way. Assured by locals that no trains were due for a half hour, Weston went bounding across without the least hesitation, but he had second thoughts and became very nervous very quickly. What if the locals were off in their calculations? If a train approached, there was no way to escape beyond leaping into the water 150 feet below. In nearly a half century of walking—and forty-three days into this journey—the old pedestrian had faced and conquered everything from blizzards, sandstorms, and intense heat to snappy dogs and Confederate posses. But he had never faced the danger of going head-to-head with a speeding train on a railroad trestle, the prospect of which caused him an old-fashioned panic attack. "I experienced a shock that seemingly overpowered my faculties," Weston said later. "In case a train approached I had no way to escape except to jump in the river. I got very nervous and was getting dizzy."

No trains passed. A nervous Weston got to the western side of the trestle. Back on the tracks again, he found the roadbed in terrible condition and hard slogging for several more miles. By the next day, Wednesday, May 5, a bright sun without wind sent temperatures soaring as Weston on all of four hours of sleep trudged the thirty-one miles from Higginsville to Oak Grove, just east of Kansas City. But here, as throughout Missouri and seemingly everywhere else, the old pedestrian continually went to his ace in the hole—utilizing his enduring fame and an ability to connect with just about everyone—to help meet his needs. The crowds that met Weston at the edge of their towns and walked with him were becoming increasingly important to the old pedestrian. They were a buffer against the loneliness and hardships of the prairie.

Also of assistance was the attention of railroad men, among the blue-collar workers with whom Weston had always enjoyed a strong bond, such as he did with law-enforcement officials. Similar to E. O. Kelly, station agent of the Wabash Railroad, those railroad men were there to lavish the walkist with help, much of which was sorely needed throughout the state. In Mexico, Missouri, another Wabash Railroad official, named Frank Bruton, threw a dinner in Weston's honor at the Hoxs-eye Hotel. Outside Marshall, following his nerve-racking tres-tle episode, two trains roared by and whistled their greetings as passengers hung from windows and shouted their own regards. On May 4 near Kansas City, another trainman threw a bottle toward Weston with a message inside. "We wish you a pleas-ant trip . . . and hope you have success in the great task you have undertaken," it said. No wonder Weston so cherished these relationships.

. . .

After the multitude of hardships of the open road in Mis-souri, Kansas City felt like a trip to the spa. Though it was chilly again Friday, May 6, as Weston strolled the thirty-two miles from Oak Grove into the city, the old pedestrian basked in the attention of the crowds gathered to see him. Edging ever closer to town, he was struck by the abundance of good roads, sunshine, and "all the comforts of home," as he put it. In Independence, Weston was serenaded by crowds that filled automobiles, as 250 Independence High School students lined the street in greeting their famous visitor. There was no word, however, whether one resident—a twenty-four-year-old farmer, 1901 high school graduate, and member of the Missouri Air National Guard named Harry Truman—was there. Thought to be working the family farm several towns away in Grand-view at the time, the future president most likely skipped the big event.

At the Metropolitan Hotel in Independence, Weston stopped for a bowl of oatmeal and then rested on a cot while chatting with reporters. Fifty minutes later he was headed down West Maple Street for the final leg into Kansas City. Moving at a steady clip of four miles per hour, he was accompanied by members of the Kansas City Hiking Club, who, unlike a lot of local walk-ers, presumably were able to stay abreast with their esteemed fellow pedestrian. Twice more, students from local schools gathered on the street to send him best wishes, to which the walkist theatrically bowed his appreciation. "It does me more good than anything else to have these children greet me," he said. "It cheers me and makes my journey easier."

That last leg was more than an old man out for a walk. It was a celebration of the human spirit, a coronation for a living leg-end trying to do something extraordinary. Heading west along Fifteenth Street, Weston and his hiking friends were met by an escort of mounted policemen without whom the crush gath-ered to greet them "would have been uncontrollable," reported the *Kansas City Journal*. All in all, it was a scene, at the cen-ter of which was Weston, "a most picturesque character," as the newspaper called him, clad in a white shirt fringed with embroidery at the neck and wrist, plaid walking trousers sus-pended by a wide belt, and hiking shoes. "His dress does just what he wishes it to do—attract attention," the *Journal* added. "He shows his 70 years only by his wheat head and a dropping white mustache." Otherwise, the walk had all the familiarities of a Weston trek—the gait with which he moved forward while weaving slightly from side to side and the steady pace that left more than a few locals in the dust.

Arriving at 4:45 p.m. at the Coates House Hotel, where he would spend the evening, Weston was neither "travel worn nor weary," the *Journal* noted, and once again in a buoyant mood. "It was the greatest day of the trip to date," the pedestrian said, meaning it for the next day or two at least. "Never have I been so royally received. And never on any of my jaunts have I traveled such roads and passed through such beautiful country as I did today. I will never forget this day and the kind people of Kansas City."

9

"Make a Good Record First and Meet Me After"

By late February 1868, Weston's calendar was filling up. On February 22 he gave what was billed as a "Walk and Talk" in Titusville, Pennsylvania, northeast of Pittsburgh; and despite heavy snow, the event sold out.

On March 27 Weston traveled to St. James Hall in Buffalo as what was billed as "part of a grand entertainment for the benefit of the poor." Eight days later, he won a bet by finally hitting the century—tramping 103 miles from near Erie, Pennsylvania, back to Buffalo in twenty-three hours and fifty-eight minutes, beating the deadline by two minutes. An enormous crowd greeted Weston as he arrived at the finish line at the post office after tramping over muddy roads and through a snowstorm. But did he arrive just in time for dramatic effect? An eyewitness described him as "looking as fresh as a lark." Weston wasn't saying.

With George K. Goodwin continuing as Weston's business manager, the purses were lucrative—some on the books and others off. But every task was a challenge, usually subject to the elements and each one seemingly more difficult than the previous one. In cases involving prize money, Weston either won the reward or didn't; in bets, however, he stood to make a lot or lose everything. On June 4 at Riverside Park in Boston, Weston wagered he could walk one hundred miles, not in twenty-four hours but *twenty-three*. A crowd of five thousand, probably not watching all twenty-three hours, were there to cheer him on, and a brass band provided entertainment. But Weston failed, covering *only* ninety and a half miles before packing it in after twenty-two hours and fifty-two minutes and having to cough up more than $4,000 on the outcome.

That must have hurt, but the fact that Weston didn't always succeed only expanded his popularity. Here was a sports hero who was mortal, someone you rooted for like a great boxer or a jockey who triumphed sometimes but often did not. It was only a matter of time before America's newest sports star attracted competitors from Britain, where pedestrianism had been popular for decades. Slightly more than two weeks following his Riverside Park walk, Weston took on English champion George Topley in a one-hundred-miler in Boston, in what appeared to be the first head-to-head competition. As part of the $3,000 purse, the first man to reach twenty-five miles would earn the first $1,000 of the prize, which the Englishman easily took, by a mile in fact. But Weston wasn't discouraged and, as the hours rolled by, steadily chipped ever closer to his opponent. Topley felt the pressure and, after taking a break at the seventy-four-mile mark, decided he couldn't make it another step. Weston was triumphant.

There were other challengers, not all of whom Weston beat. Cornelius Payn of Albany triumphed August 22 in a one-hundred-mile contest on a half-mile circular track at Rensselear Park in Troy, New York, after Weston, ahead by more than a mile, withdrew after eighty-one miles because of fever. Payn beat him again at one hundred miles in early September at Troy, after which Weston complained he found it difficult to compete on circular tracks. That probably sounded odd, stated in the disappointment just after finishing. But the "walkist," as Weston was increasingly being called, was becoming ever more popular, as much for his breezy self-confidence as for his remarkable athleticism. On October 8 Weston set a world record for walking one hundred miles, arriving at the Orawarhum Hotel in White Plains, New York, in a resounding twenty-two hours, nineteen minutes, and eight seconds, beating the old mark by forty minutes. Addressing the crowd, Weston was charmingly succinct: "The walk was made with little difficulty with no apparent ill effects."

In late 1868 Weston was offered his greatest potential purse yet—$20,000 to walk some five thousand miles from Bangor, Maine, to St. Paul and then back east to New York in one hundred days. An odometer would gauge his daily distance, and two horse-drawn carriages would carry supplies. So the great pedestrian pushed off on December 4, trudging through all the usual snowstorms, uneven roads, and storms of attention. It was quite a show on the evening of January 30, 1869, when a man adorned in a military uniform and followed by three horse sleighs passed briskly through Burlington, Vermont, hailed by the mayor and feted by the townspeople who lit his way with celebratory bonfires. They had seen the great Weston, or so it seemed. That Weston was a fake, a goof cooked up and carried out by a clever group of local college students. Imagine the surprise of the real Weston when he came barreling through town the next day. Informed of the hoax, he was "much annoyed by the sham," according to press reports.

Weston's schedule depended on covering fifty miles a day. Excitement followed his every step. Near Syracuse, church-goers were so excited to see him walk by that they ran out of a prayer meeting, "leaving the pious parson alone," a reporter wrote. But trudging through the sometimes waist-deep snows of upstate New York was problematic at best, and Weston fell farther and farther behind. Abandoning his quest in Buffalo, he refused to blame the weather for his troubles but said he had stopped because he had run out of money in part because more people hadn't invited him to stay overnight in their homes. In total, Weston covered 1,153 miles in thirty-six days, proving both that the odometer had worked like a charm and that he was human after all.

. . .

Pedestrianism was a rough-and-tumble business in those days. Gamblers were everywhere, setting the odds, throwing out occasional threats, and putting some results in doubt. Charges of cheating were frequent. Challengers came and went—and some who couldn't beat Weston called him a fraud or a cheat, a "humbug" in the vernacular of the day. So intent was Weston to prove his feats were legitimate that on May 25, 1870, he submitted himself to the scrutiny of seven judges, vowing to achieve the unparalleled feat of walking one hundred miles at the Empire Skating Rink in New York City, not in twenty-four hours, but in *twenty-two*. Weston was confident he could do it, telling reporters that if not, he would "die in the attempt." Heaven knows how those judges lasted all that time—it was determined that Weston would need to circle the course laid around the rink more than 718 times. But the judges were there along with five thousand people on hand to witness the great walkist achieve his goal. Making nine rest stops, each less than ten minutes, Weston crossed the threshold in an astounding twenty-one hours, thirty-eight minutes, and fifteen seconds, proving that he had a knack for circular tracks after all and that he most certainly wasn't a humbug. "Mr. Weston did not seem in the least fatigued by, stepping off as briskly on the last mile as on the first," the *New York Herald* wrote, "and after the 100th mile had been accomplished, he addressed the crowd from the judge's stand, saying that it was love, not money, which had induced him to attempt the feat which he had just accomplished."

That seemed accurate. "Money was an important factor, but it wasn't Weston's prime motivation," said Paul S. Marshall, an expert on Victorian pedestrianism and the author of the authoritative book on the subject, *King of the Peds.* "Weston was a determined, gutsy individual who wanted to win at all costs. . . . Failure to him was the worst thing that could happen."

So Weston walked around rinks and at county fairs. He gave public exhibitions in which he walked and talked about it afterward. Sometimes he even walked backward for long distances—as he did in his two-hundred-mile circuit of St. Louis in 1871—explaining that it relaxed his legs, especially on downgrades. Doing so earned him more headlines and a rash of nicknames, such as the Wily Wobbler and the Yankee Clipper, decades before Joe DiMaggio took the moniker. Often, he was Weston the Walker or simply Weston, in the same spirit as more recent athletic heroes, who seem to be referred to by single names only. Refer to "Jordan," "Pujols," or "Brady," and sports fans will probably know whom you're talking about. It helped Weston's persona that he was opinionated, dashing, and exceedingly distinctive. For newspaper reporters, Weston wasn't just a man walking through town; he was *a happening.* In Rutland, Vermont, a local reporter described his attire as tight-fitting breeches held up by a tightly clasped belt, a short roundabout jacket, a small military cap on his head, and a fancy riding whip, which he held "for company or amusement." Another account had Weston adorned in buff gloves and "high shoes with red tops."

Weston hired a trainer, Charles Winnans, and together the two men explored nutrition and new racing strategies to help him walk faster. Attempting in June 1871 to walk four hundred miles in five days in New York, Weston decided to rest just forty-five minutes in his first twenty-four hours and afterward for five minutes every twenty-five miles. Dressed for part of the trek in a velvet suit and a blue sash, Weston made his deadline by eighteen minutes, covering the last miles in a speedy eleven minutes and seven seconds, while "show[ing] little signs of fatigue," the *Washington Patriot* reported. That autumn at the

Georgia State Fair, Weston gave some insight into his training regimen, telling the *Atlanta Constitution* that for a month leading into a long walk, he would stop smoking and refrain from salt, meat, and for some reason, parsnips. At the age of thirty-two, Weston professed his diet worked wonders, giving him a solid competitive advantage. The man from the *Constitution* was impressed as much by the pedestrian's accomplishments and appearance—seeming "much younger" than his age—as by his manners, which were "polished and easy . . . with a ceaseless flow of spirits and humor."

Weston's status grew, and so did the competition. Some were pretenders, but the man who most threatened Weston's records was Daniel O'Leary, an Irish farmer who had settled in Chicago. On July 15, 1874, O'Leary walked one hundred miles in twenty-three hours and seventeen minutes—not quite up to Weston's mark but strong enough that he issued a challenge to the great pedestrian. The bad blood started immediately with Weston refusing the offer, telling the Irishman to "make a good record first and meet me after." So O'Leary did, setting out to walk five hundred miles around a Chicago rink in 156 hours, which he bested by nearly two and a half hours.

O'Leary was the real deal, a twenty-nine-year-old County Cork native who had arrived in New York just after the Civil War. Not finding work there, he picked cotton in Mississippi and then headed to Chicago, where he ran a Bible store. Walking out of a dry goods store in Chicago one day in 1873, O'Leary overheard a conversation that would change his life.

"None but a Yankee can perform such a feat," said one man, addressing Weston's goal to walk five hundred miles in six days.

"Hold on, hold on," countered O'Leary, unable to help himself. "Perhaps a foreigner might do it."

"He won't be an Irishman," chimed in another, baiting him.

O'Leary stayed calm. "Ireland has sent forth some good men," he suggested hopefully.

The others weren't convinced. "Wonderful fellows, indeed," one replied sarcastically. "They can accomplish almost anything with their tongues."

O'Leary kept his composure. "The tongue is the mean member of the human frame," he said. "Had Cicero and Demosthenes been born dumb, two great minds would have passed away from earth to eternity, like the bird flying through the air, without leaving a trace of their greatness behind."

Cicero and Demosthenes? The story sounds apocryphal, but it's a good one. According to O'Leary, the men began to titter, enough so that he decided right then and there to never sell another Bible in his life and become a pedestrian. "Laugh as you please, gentlemen," he told them, "but bear in mind that I will beat Weston in a fair contest."

And so he did. O'Leary and Weston faced off at the Exposition Building in New York on November 15, 1875, in a six-day match race that was practically over before it started. Starting off at a comfortable pace, not yet pushing himself, Weston let O'Leary take a commanding lead, thinking he would resort to his usual late kick. The race was the spectacle of its day, albeit a slow-moving one that seems a bit odd today. Each walker stuck to his lane and took a break up to forty-five minutes at a time to eat, change clothes, and get a rub down. At night, the walkers slept for three to four hours, usually around midnight. Crowds came and went but, owing perhaps to the mind-numbing tedium of watching two men walk in circles for hours on end, never exceeded four hundred. Weston couldn't catch up and after six days was a mind-boggling forty-eight miles behind O'Leary. The world had a new champion walker, but the rivalry was just getting started.

. . .

It was inevitable that Weston would head to London, long the bastion of pedestrianism. Sailing in January 1876 for Great

Britain, he wasted little time in finding a crowd up for a challenge. So who was this American upstart who had nearly walked five hundred miles in six days? the British press asked. Posing the question and promptly answering themselves, they made up their minds: walking nearly five hundred miles in six days wasn't possible. It was simply too fantastic to be true.

They would soon change their minds. On February 8, 1876, William Perkins, a twenty-four-year-old Londoner and the only Englishman to have walked eight miles in an hour, challenged Weston to a twenty-four-hour race around the track at Agricultural Hall in the Islington section of London. Though the winner would earn sixty pounds and a silver cup, the real reward would be more lucrative paydays to come.

Weston exuded an easy confidence, speculating he might cover as many as 115 miles within the designated time. Dressing in a matching velvet jacket and trousers—the jogging suit of its day—which he topped off with a sparkling blue sash, a raffish, low-slung white leather hat, and his trademark whip in hand, the thirty-seven-year-old American seemed neither nervous nor excitable. Perkins, who was younger and clearly faster than Weston, raced to an immediate lead—fifty-seven seconds after a mile. Steadily stretching his advantage, the Englishman was sixty-one minutes ahead at twenty miles and fifty-one minutes up at thirty miles. Perkins appeared so confident that he then took a break for dinner, a warm bath, and a change of shoes.

Weston never took a break, using a whistle to summon a trainer with a smorgasbord of refreshing products from jelly to beef tea, egg yolks, and chunks of ice. He cut the distance somewhat—Perkins was now forty-nine minutes in front at fifty miles—but the American was counting on the Englishman, who had never competed in anything close to a twenty-four-hour race, not being able to maintain the pace. He was right, and a little short of the sixty-mile mark, Perkins checked in for treatment of his badly swollen feet. Back to it, he stumbled along painfully for another six miles or so before finally packing it in after fourteen hours and sixty-five miles. Perkins was in bad shape: his pulse and temperature were up, and his blood pressure down. And his feet were so swollen that attendants had to cut off his boots.

Meanwhile, Weston kept on walking, taking only a single break at the seventy-mile mark and seemingly intent on convincing the public and press alike that he was the pedestrian to beat. Hitting the century mark at nineteen hours and twenty minutes, he reached 109 miles after twenty-four hours, a result so impressive that the audience lined the track and cheered. But apparently, beef extract and egg yolks weren't the only things Weston had consumed during the race. When reporters found out that he had also chewed cocoa leaves, the raw material for the manufacture of cocaine, it caused a sensation.

Weston never denied ingesting cocoa, stating in a letter to the *British Medical Journal* that he didn't think it helped him at all during the race and in fact made him groggy. Though Weston's performance wasn't disputed, the controversy was the 1876 version of today's steroids debate. Even then, the connection between coca leaves and performance was widely accepted; as such, race walkers would still be chewing the leaves a decade later. In 1885 Dr. E. R. Palmer, a cocoa advocate from Louisville, Kentucky, published a report of a pedestrian trying to walk 350 miles in seven days, who went from a state of near collapse to revival after drinking a glass of Fraser's Wine of Coca.

Did Weston's use of cocoa brand him as a cheater? Maybe so, but chances are the American would have won anyway. Was he a habitual drug user? That was doubtful considering he said it made him sleepy. And considering his conscientiousness in removing even the whiff of rule breaking combined with his instance on alcohol control and a healthy diet, it's likely that

Weston was an infrequent user and, after the controversy, never again touched the stuff.

. . .

It wasn't long before Weston and O'Leary met again. To reporters, they had become the two greats of pedestrianism—the Ali versus Frazier of the day, big-time rivals looking to score big paydays and assume the mantle of the "best." They were a publicist's dream, an intriguing study in contrasts: the established but occasional herky-jerky gait of Weston against the younger O'Leary and his more traditional, straight-up style. Weston was great fodder, quotable with opinions on this, that, and everything. And though O'Leary wasn't nearly as interesting, he had his own quirks, namely his curious habit of clutching a corn cob in each hand as he walked. "A habit as much as anything else," he told the *New York Sun* of his cob carrying. "They . . . absorb the perspiration and keep the hands from swelling . . . a light grip on them seemed to make me solid." Information like that was news in Great Britain, where interest in pedestrianism was off the charts—a spectator sport of remarkable interest among not just the "toffs" of the old days but the middle and lower classes as well.

Of the two, Weston drew the most attention. To the English press, he wasn't just another walker, but "the renowned American pedestrian." And that was only the beginning. Preparing to walk in Edinburgh, Scotland, Weston pushed the public relations practitioners into overdrive, as this attention-screaming poster attests:

TODAY! TODAY!! TODAY!!!
THE GREATEST ENDURER LIVING!
EDWARD PAYSON WESTON,

The Most Wonderful Illustrator of Long Distance pedestrianism and almost Superhuman Endurance—from Scientific

Living—the World has ever known, has been Engaged at
GREAT EXPENSE *by the Lessee of the*

ROYAL GYMNASIUM

To give one of his unique and exciting Illustrations

In Edinburgh, on Friday the 26th inst.,
    When with an easy, unbroken, and apparently careless gait,
he will without a rest, WALK *within* TWELVE CONSECUTIVE
HOURS *a Distance of 55 miles, including a half mile backward.*
A Splendid Band will be in attendance . . . To accommodate
the many Thousands of anxious Spectators to this, the Only
Entertainment to be given in Edinburgh by Mr. WESTON, *the*
Lessee had decided to place the admission at the low price of
Sixpence, with only Sixpence extra to the Reserved Seats.

Finally, Weston went head-to-head against O'Leary in a
rematch, in April 1877 in a storied six-day race at Agricultural
Hall in London. Reporters sized them up like two heavyweights
and emphasized their contrasts, with one calling O'Leary "the
perfect opposite of Weston." Whereas "the latter [Weston] is
talkative and demonstrative; the former [O'Leary] is taciturn,
and seems to shun notoriety," the report continued. "When
walking a match, Weston wears a showy dress and flourishes a
gold-handled riding whip; O'Leary, when on the track, dresses
very plainly, and carries a corn cob in each hand. Weston craves
public applause, and is extremely sensitive to outside remarks;
O'Leary plods along apparently without interest in spectators,
and neither gibe nor applause affects his gait."

Their contrasting walking techniques drew attention. The
London Times described O'Leary's style as "statuesque," one
that "quite comes up to an Englishman's idea of what walking
should be." On the other hand, the paper stated, Weston has "a
very peculiar jerky gait, which is the reverse of graceful . . . his
short 'springy' step . . . quite different from that of O'Leary."

Excitement ran high. There were six judges for the six-day race, including a former British sea captain named Matthew Webb, the first man to conquer the English Channel. Webb was a good choice, adding a dash of real star appeal to the competition. Slathered in porpoise oil to retain his body heat and trailed by three boats, the captain in August 1875 had left Admiralty Pier in Dover and headed toward Cap Gris Nez, France. Stung by jellyfish, he plowed toward his dream and emerged from the waters after twenty-one hours and, because of the strong currents, closer to Calais. His challenging journey wasn't the twenty-two miles he had envisioned but a shade under forty.

Some seventy thousand paying spectators took in the pedestrian spectacle. Unlike their tussle back in New York, Weston kept it close; but in the end, O'Leary won again, this time breaking his own six-day record by covering 519 miles, 21 miles ahead of Weston. The competitors split the gate, with each receiving $14,000—the equivalent of more than $300,000 today. "It was a good week's work," O'Leary said, with no apparent irony. But it was anything but a good week's work for a certain member of Parliament who was reported to have lost £20,000 by betting on Weston; he and the American would later develop a long and lucrative connection.

Weston may have lost, but his star didn't dim at all. Ever gracious, he blamed himself for his loss, admitting in a letter to the *Scotsman* newspaper that he had underrated O'Leary's powers of endurance and challenging O'Leary to a further set of races. But that wouldn't happen for a while, because in May, O'Leary sailed back to the United States and went home to Chicago. Weston, in the meantime, stayed on in the United Kingdom, where he was lavished by eighty-seven members of Parliament with a banquet at the Westminster Palace Hotel.

One of the ministers that night at dinner was Sir John Astley, the man who lost all that money but had become so captivated by the great O'Leary-Weston match race that he proposed a rather grand sequel of his own. A onetime member of the elite Scots Fusilier Guards, Astley had served in the Crimean War, retired as a lieutenant colonel, and married an heiress. Retirement was good to Sir John, a tweedy-looking, gregarious chap known familiarly as "the Mate" and well-known for winning and losing vast sums at racetracks and boxing arenas. Astley's proposal was a series of six-day races to be called the Astley Belt, for the mantle as "Long Distance Champion of the World," with any man taking the race three times in a row permanently taking the belt. So in March 1878 back to Agricultural Hall headed O'Leary and seventeen others, all from England, Ireland, and Scotland to try for the first one.

O'Leary won that first race and the second. Looking to take the third race and retire the belt, O'Leary lost to Charles Rowell, a defeat so devastating that he was driven into a premature but temporary retirement. Though he was living in Great Britain, Weston wasn't a part of those first three competitions, content to walk and lecture on his own. In early 1879 Weston embarked on a truly epic cross-country excursion—attempting to walk two thousand miles around Great Britain in one thousand hours while delivering fifty lectures en route. Lecturing provided some additional income, as would collecting on a £100 bet from Astley, who had laid five-to-one odds that Weston wouldn't make it. Weston very nearly did amid the cold and gloom of the British winter, falling all of twenty-two and a half miles short. So Weston lost his bet, but he cleared several hundred pounds with his lectures and brisk sales of photos and walking pamphlets.

Was Weston avoiding O'Leary? Possibly. But there were simply too many lucrative solo walks and lectures for the offing. At Northumberland Cricket Ground in Newcastle, Weston performed one of his most stupendous feats of all—covering one thousand miles in four hundred hours, which included his fastest mile of all, the 995th mile in nine minutes and fifteen seconds, faster than many could run. The crossover star of his time, Weston attracted "all shades of men, the clergy, the medical profession, and the lower orders of society," the *Newcastle Daily Chronicle* wrote. "A large number of ladies patronised Weston's tent, the polished manners and unrestrained gaiety of Weston rendering him a great favourite with his lady patrons."

Sir John Astley had just about given up on Weston ever entering his competition. But there was the forty-year-old American pedestrian lining up for the start of the fourth Astley Belt on March 5, 1879, back at Agricultural Hall. Although O'Leary wasn't there, Charles Rowell and another British champion, Blower Brown, were, and so was John Ennis of Chicago. As usual, Weston let others take the lead, but by the second day he had dropped to a strong second in sticking doggedly to Brown. Halfway through day three, Weston grabbed the lead and during a break announced to reporters that, should he go on to win, it would be his farewell race in Great Britain. Late that night, Weston was twenty-five miles in front and already celebrating, telling Astley with a laugh that "I am going to do my level best to take your belt back to the States."

Weston did his level best, taking the £500 prize along with £132 in gate receipts and another £500 stake from Astley for passing the 550-mile mark in world-record time. Marking the event with a flourish by carrying British and American flags during his last lap, Weston was again on top. His victory was so improbable that charges flew of Weston deliberately laying low well into the race in order to skew the odds for an extra big payoff. But insiders knew that they had seen something extraordinary.

Ennis, who dropped out of the competition after 180 miles, attributed Weston's victory to a new dedication to his sport and smart strategy. "For the first time since I have known him, he went on the track to win and not to win the admiration of the ladies," Ennis said. That meant discarding his usual frilly shirt and theatrical sash for a more athletic pair of tights, thin white undershirt, and ordinary trunks—an outfit suited for walking "and not simply to make a show of himself," he added. And it meant indulging in some head games by turning around at one point and walking in reverse to break the spirit of the main pursuer, Blower Brown. "I don't mean to say that Weston would not have won the race anyway . . . but I do say that Brown's performance would have been better but for these tactics," observed Ennis. Nor was Astley buying the tales of deceit. To Sir John, Weston was "one who has striven to teach the world what the powers of man are capable of when governed by pluck, perseverance, and abstinence from overindulgence in the so-called pleasures of dissipation." Weston and Astley weren't so much friends as mutual admirers, men who recognized that maintaining a strong relationship could be beneficial for both. So it was in 1879 when Astley was getting slammed in the British press by editorial writers convinced he was exploiting Weston and even assuring his early death that the walkist leaped to his defense.

Astley wasn't killing him, Weston scoffed. Nor was he goading him, he insisted. So superior was his overall physical condition due to walking that the forty-year-old Weston pledged right then and there that that in thirty years when he was seventy, he would foot it clear across the United States, coast-to-coast from New York to San Francisco. Moreover, he would complete the 3,900-mile trek in one hundred days. The task, he said, "would make all previous efforts look small in comparison." Nobody thought much about that at the time, but exactly thirty years later, in 1909, there was Weston sticking to the plan, a man of his word.

. . .

Edward Payson Weston had another surprise in store after winning the Astley Belt. Returning in the late summer of 1879 to

Madison Square Garden in New York to defend his title in the fifth annual Belt, Weston lost to Charles Rowell. But within days, Weston and his wife, Maria, were headed back to Europe, where they would remain for most of the next four years.

Weston and Maria lived in Britain and France from 1876 to 1884. For the most part, the couple's three children spent most of those years living with Maria's parents in Stamford, Connecticut, though in 1882 their eldest daughter, Lillian, moved to London to attend school. In the meantime, Weston continued to put his own needs first, well ahead of his family—only occasionally communicating with his children, coming and going as he wished, and sticking to his own agenda. Forever outgoing and never cruel or abusive, he was still at times "a bit of a tyrant" to his family, his great-granddaughter Joyce Litz claimed. "His likes, his comforts and his ideas came first," at the expense of his wife and children, she added, which often meant staying up all night and sleeping all day. Weston "didn't adjust his life to suit anyone else, an attitude bound to sour a relationship," Litz wrote. "He had his own ideas on all subjects and paid little attention to other people's opinions."

Other pedestrians came and went. But by the mid-1870s, to Americans, walking started and finished with one person: Weston. Many shared the late Henry David Thoreau's passion for walking—among them was the author and humorist Mark Twain of Hartford, Connecticut. An avid pedestrian, Twain and his pastor Joseph Twichell enjoyed making regular eight-mile excursions to Talcott Mountain while talking and forging a strong friendship in the process. Forever in search of comic material, often with himself as the foil, Twain in November 1874 set out with Twichell on a well-publicized one-hundred-mile trek to Boston. He joked that he was competing with Weston.

Twain and Twichell "would show their independence of the cars, and notify Mr. Weston, the great walkist, that he must look to his laurels," wrote Peter Messent, author of *Mark Twain and Male Friendship: The Twichell, Howells, and Rogers Friend-ships*. Not surprisingly, the whole episode became something of a farce. After twenty-eight miles, Twain's knee had stiffened, and the two men decided to cover the rest of the distance in a more comfortable manner. "It was as though I had wooden legs with pains in them," Twain wrote of his knee troubles. So completing their journey by horse and cart and finally by rail, Twain made comic capital of the excursion's failure. "We have made thirty-five miles in less than five days," he telegraphed his Boston lecture agent. "This demonstrates the thing can be done. Shall now finish by rail. Did you have any bets on us?"

Everybody chuckled at the uncomfortable journey of Twain, who had recently won renown for his book *Innocents Abroad*. The press feasted on Twain and Twichell's adventure. "It has long been the custom of these two gentlemen to take walks of about 10 miles in the vicinity of Hartford for the purpose of enjoying a social chat and exchanging views on nothing in particular and everything in general," the *Windham County (CT) Transcript* wrote. "The result of which [is] . . . that Mr. Twichell sometimes gains ideas from his companion which he embodies in his sermon, and Mark Twain obtains information from his pastor which he works into comical and humorous stories, and makes note of every joke which unfortunately falls from the clerical lips."

Twain reveled in the episode. His friend, the author William Dean Howells, greeted the two men in Boston with a party in their honor. As Twichell noted in his diary, "Got back to Young's [hotel] at 1 o'clock and went joy-filled to bed." Next, Twain hosted a dinner for his Boston friends—"a rare good time which I enjoyed to the full," Twichell wrote. "Heard lots of bright good talk." Describing their journey home, Twichell called it, "on some accounts the most pleasant experience of my life. . . . There has been no end of talk in the press about our 'tour.'"

10

"Some Command of the Situation"

Folding a map of the continental United States in half vertically creases it smack dab in the middle of Kansas. Based on data furnished by the U. S. Coast and Geodetic Survey, a speck of a town named Lebanon—population 218—in north-central Kansas, is the geographical center of the Lower 48. Today there is even a plaque, courtesy of the Lebanon Hub Club, to commemorate the unusual distinction, situated a half mile north of town off Highway 281 in the middle of a former hog farm. "There really isn't very much to see or do at the Geographical Center of the United States," advises the Kansas Travel and Tourism website. "But if you are passing through the area on U.S. highways 36 or 281, it is worth driving the short distance from Lebanon."

Weston wouldn't pass through Lebanon. Trekking due west from Kansas City, he would be headed directly across the center of the state—"the heart of the heartland"—and the halfway point of his great walk across America. By going this route, he would be taking in several of the state's biggest and most significant cities, including Lawrence, home of the University of Kansas; Manhattan, the location of Fort Riley; and Topeka, the state capital. But for the most part, his walk was through sparsely populated parts of the state and a preview of what lay ahead: rapidly changing weather coupled with the challenge of having to cover increasingly greater distances between towns.

Kansas is flat, flat as a board, which triggers all kinds of sudden weather complications. On the Great Plains, rains can swoop in fiercely and rage for days. So do tornados, high winds, and searing heat. For Weston, there was no real preparation beyond remembering to drink and eat regularly, resting periodically, and finding shelter when it was available, all while trying to stay in touch with his manager. This was also the point where Weston reached an important strategic decision— heading back to the railroad beds for good. He would follow the roadbed of the Union Pacific Railroad after all.

Leaving the Coates Hotel in Kansas City at 5:00 a.m. on Friday, May 7, for the fifty-five-mile trip to Perry, Weston was already at a disadvantage. The hotel dining room opened at 6:00 a.m., too late for his purposes, so he arranged for an early breakfast of milk and oatmeal, lighter than usual but the best he could do at that hour. Also, manager John Schinkel was ill and would stay behind for the time being. At least Weston had some companionship, a *Kansas City Star* reporter and one R. R. Collins of the Bell Telephone Company, along for the adventure and not in an official capacity. That was fortunate because three hours out of Kansas City, Weston began paying for his light breakfast, becoming powerfully hungry— "so hungry I became faint," he said. Up stepped Collins, who strode ahead to the hamlet of Muncie on the north bank of the Kansas River near Kansas City, Kansas, to act as a surrogate manager—finding a Good Samaritan to provide emergency rations. This time, the star stranger of the hour turned out to be one C. F. Hahn, who came through with a hearty breakfast that helped Weston revive himself and make it the rest of the way to Perry. A major tip of the hat went to R. R. Collins for having aided Weston at a moment of need *and* covering thirty-two miles Friday without stopping. "He is the best amateur pedestrian I have had to accompany me on this trip," said the professional pedestrian.

On Saturday, May 8, the Kansas weather reared itself. It was pouring when Weston left Perry at 6:00 a.m., so Weston changed to rainy-day togs, which were heavy and slowed him down. Up stepped R. R. Collins for another day of adventure, intent on accompanying his new mentor for as many miles as he could manage. Even in the rain, things proceeded reasonably well, for a time at least, with crews and passengers alike cheering them from trains along the Union Pacific Railroad. The walking party proved a welcome site as well for a sizable crowd who met the walkers in Topeka, where they lunched. But back on the road for the next stage, twenty miles west to St. Mary's, Weston found himself in a bind: poor Collins had "hit the wall," the marathoner's turn of phrase for his version of being unable to make it another step. He had become violently ill—Weston never said exactly what he had—and the old pedestrian felt compelled to stay with him.

It was raining buckets anyway, so the old pedestrian would rest Sunday in Topeka, marking his total distance for the week at 239 miles. Weston had other more successful weeks, but given the myriad of hardships in the last few days, the week was hardly a total loss. His total distance for the trip after forty-eight days of walking was 1,918 miles—a shade above an average of 42 miles a day. "Reviewing my walk of the last week and the obstacles ahead which I have to overcome," Weston wrote from Topeka, "I am content in enjoying this day of rest."

. . .

Nothing further was heard of R. R. Collins. Presumably, he recovered and went home to Kansas City, grateful for his moment in the sun, demonstrating again that there are many people capable of feats of athletic endurance for a day or two but not on Weston's relentless marathon-and-more-a-day pace.

Set for his ninth week on the road, Weston had hoped to be another 200 miles or so farther along the 4,300-mile trail, but he was upbeat anyway. Back home, "my friends may feel somewhat worried, but they need have no fear," he admitted. "I am confident that I have not overrated my ability and will finish my walk in the allotted time of one hundred days."

Weston longed to get in a solid week of walking in the flatness of the corn and wheat country of Kansas. Things were looking up. John Schinkel, his manager, was feeling better and raring to go. And despite the usual morning stiffness—Weston was again walking down the stairs of hotels backward to stretch and to preserve his strength—the old pedestrian felt strong. To prove it, he sauntered seventy-two miles all the way to Junction City on Monday, Weston's most productive day of the entire trip. Even better, there was an upbeat letter from one of his New York backers—the "King of Mascots"—waiting for him in Junction City. And those crowds! They gathered in pockets all day Monday—in Manhattan and farther along at Fort Riley, where a whole gang turned out to greet Weston, including the U.S. Army base's acting commandant, the artillery colonel, and a slew of officers and their wives. And there were the crowds, again, on Tuesday, some twenty-five miles west of Junction City in Abilene, where a delegation from the Elks Club escorted Weston to lunch at the Bartell Hotel.

Weston ambled forty-two miles to New Cambria that Tuesday, walking day number fifty, but would soon need every break he could get. On Wednesday, May 12, the skies blackened and winds turned fierce, sending Weston skidding down the railroad embankment. By early afternoon, as the winds continued to howl, the skies turned hot, baking hot, a signal that summer had arrived on the plains in a heartbeat. Weston covered the forty-three miles to Ellsworth—resting in the midday heat and making up nearly half the distance in the late evening, arriving at midnight.

In the meantime, Weston was finding the Kansas plains challenging for a whole other reason. The distance between the towns was significantly farther than in the East, meaning far fewer places for shelter and food. As he did between New Cambria and Ellsworth, Weston took to resting at midday and walking more in the cool of the evenings—and in doing so, he discovered the powerful darkness in which the only light radiates from the stars, the kind of enveloping blackness seldom experienced in the East. And though Weston was free of injury for the time being, that changed in a heartbeat on Thursday, May 13; when leaving Ellsworth, he felt such intense pain in his left heel that he thought at first a nail had worn through his shoe. It wasn't a nail; it was a small stone that wedged into the shoe on Tuesday and into Weston's heel. Considering the old pedestrian had just passed the two-thousand-mile mark of his great trek westward, it's remarkable—and probably doubtful—that this was the first substantial injury he had suffered from a stone, rock, or nail.

The day really never got much better. Pushing off at 11:00 a.m., Weston was still sore heading into the day's most intense heat. Three miles west of town, he was resting when a farmer spotted him and took him to his house to await cooler temperatures. Back on the road just after 1:00 p.m., Weston was still limping, so one and a half miles up the road, he rested under a railroad bridge. Some three and a half miles later, he packed it in for the day at the wonderfully named hamlet of Black Wolf on the north bank of the Smoky Hill River.

For everything that Weston had learned about what it took to walk long distances, he was a realist and knew how quickly conditions or circumstances could derail the best laid plans. After a half century of experience, Weston knew himself well—when it was best to push on or to stop and leave his better efforts for another day. Having covered only eight miles on his fifty-second day of walking, by far his shortest daily distance to date, he was holing up in what was probably the route's smallest town yet. Black Wolf—with a population one hundred—boasted a grain elevator, a coal mine, and a lumber yard. There was a hotel, a general store, a bank, a telegraph, and a livery stable as well. The town even had a baseball team, which played Sundays in a cow pasture, and a big wooden barn where Saturday-night dances in the loft wouldn't end until the sun went up Sunday, so people could find their way home. Sadly, Black Wolf is no more. With better roads and cars, people began driving into Ellsworth to shop, and the little town lost its few retailers. When the Union Pacific Railroad depot closed in 1952, it was the end for Black Wolf. Today, it is one of thousands of midwestern ghost towns and a poignant reminder that the route traveled by Edward Payson Weston across America in 1909 marks a vanished place.

Black Wolf offered few dining or cultural attractions. Unfortunately, he wasn't there on a Saturday for the regularly scheduled barn dance. But a good night's sleep worked wonders, and on Friday, May 15, Weston hoofed thirty-three miles west to Russell. Still feeling strong on Saturday, May 16, despite lingering pains in his left heel and a thirty-minute cyclone near Bunker Hill, the old pedestrian closed out the week by trudging *sixty miles* all the way to WaKeeney. The knots of welcoming townspeople en route in Hays and Ellis helped to alleviate the sometimes crushing loneliness of the road. Weston's overall fitness, sore heel and all, was also improving. In the meantime, there was something else Weston wanted people to know: he was right on schedule.

"Having fully recovered from the stone bruise on [his] heel," Weston vowed to finish his daily walks by 10:00 p.m., thereby limiting the number of dark nights. Firing back at a report in a Salina, Kansas, newspaper that said he was 140 miles behind schedule, the walkist said that he was in fact "ahead of the time necessary" to reach San Francisco by July 9, day one hundred.

"My old friends in New York will realize that all my hard work was done in March and April, when I encountered blizzards, freezing roads, snowdrifts, and mud knee deep," he continued. "I am getting stronger and stronger. Whereas in March it was difficult to walk ten or fifteen miles without a rest, now I go between eighteen and twenty miles without resting."

Yes, he could. Tramping along the railroad tracks was working. The routes between towns were often more direct than roads and seldom washed out in rainstorms. Dust wasn't a problem because rail companies slathered many of the tracks in oil. No wonder Weston produced his strongest week yet in Kansas. Covering 277 miles, for a total of 2,195 miles to date, made him feel like his old self. "My many well-wishers . . . will readily realize that after forty-five years' experience in this exercise," Weston said, "I have some command of the situation."

That command was dependent on knowing when to press and when not to while keeping an overall sense of balance. Alternating hard and easy days is a staple of today's distance-running regimen, but it was novel thinking in Weston's day. So there was the pedestrian resting on Sunday, May 16, thinking that if he were going to make it from western Kansas all the way to California, he had better stick to that strategy, which would include easy Mondays, beginning after Chicago. But there he was in the dawn of Monday, May 17, feeling strong enough to make an exception. Taking advantage of how he felt, he put in one of the longest days yet of his trek across America—sixty-six miles from WaKeeney to Monument—and only then followed with an easy day. True to his word, Weston, on Tuesday, May 18, trekked only twenty-two miles to Sharon Springs, followed by a hard walk on Wednesday—heading fifty-eight miles across the Colorado state line to Cheyenne Wells.

If, on one hand, Weston was happy to leave behind the fierce weather of Kansas, the reception he had received there left a lingering impression. Headed toward the western Kansas hamlet of Buffalo Springs, now called Park, one Charles Brown of Grinnell met the great walkist with a welcome offering of home-made eggnog. The two men then headed into Buffalo Springs, where several Englishmen who had seen Weston walk years before in Bradford, England, enthusiastically greeted the old pedestrian. What those Englishmen were doing in western Kansas is lost to history; suffice it to say that Weston was just happy to see them and found the chance meeting invigorating. For a man who once carried a stick to ward off zealous fans, every encounter in this remote stretch of land where prairie dogs outnumbered people was memorable.

Weston's fame came in handy that Wednesday, May 19, shortly before crossing into Colorado. Nearing the stockyard pens of tiny Lisbon, Kansas, north of Buffalo Springs, the pedestrian slipped under a railroad platform for refuge from a nasty thunderstorm. He hadn't been there long when a local ranchman, A. C. Overhott, happened by and urged Weston to accompany him back to his home to wait out the storm. There he waited out the storm, had dinner, and spent the night, before breakfasting and heading out again. "If it had not been for the thoughtfulness of my host in coming for and urging me to go to his house I should certainly have been attacked with pneumonia or lumbago," Weston said. "I have traveled all over England and part of France and a large part of America, thus far I have never yet passed through such a beautiful and health-giving country and such genial and hospitable people as are located in the Sunflower State. To me it has been a paradise in every town and village I passed. Someone would invariably appear with some refreshing drink."

. . .

Crossing into central Colorado, Weston planned to head north-west to Denver and then directly north into Cheyenne, Wyoming. It was difficult slogging. Weston was two and a half miles east of Cheyenne Wells when it began to rain in a downpour that "came down in torrents," he said, "unlike any thunder shower in the East." Nor were there friendly railroadmen or ranchers with coffee. Drenched in three minutes, Weston had no choice beyond finding a hotel in town.

The downpour continued, so Weston remained in Cheyenne Wells Thursday, May 20, rather than heading to the road and risking illness. Back to it on Friday, May 21, in even more sparsely populated country, the pedestrian stuck to the Union Pacific Railroad tracks past small towns with spotty accommodations, "an occasional rabbit [and] many prairie dogs and coyotes," as he put it. If towns were ten miles apart in Kansas, they were even more distant in this dry, parched section of eastern Colorado, where Weston often trudged half a day without seeing another human. In Kit Carson he ate dinner in a section house—a small building for storing tools and railroad equipment—and looked on the bright side. "The rain of the last two days has had a wonderful effect on the grass and crops," he said, and "consequently everybody is industrious and cheerful."

Weston trekked forty-five miles from Cheyenne Mills to Aroya and then, on his sixtieth day of walking, twenty-eight miles to Hugo. His many contacts with railroad workers were paying off. Ten miles north of Aroya, Weston breakfasted with Owen Phillips, a section foreman at Boyero. Four miles north of there, Levin Stoner, the engineer of passenger train 109, hurled a welcome bag of ice from the cab to Weston. These were bright spots next to the couple of hobos who put a scare into Weston by actually following him for a quarter of a mile until the old walkist stepped on it and left them behind, an effort that tore a hole into his right boot. The incident underscored the loneliness that Weston sometimes faced in these desolate parts. "Then I take to thinking of . . . friends in New York and the many well-wishers elsewhere," he said.

At least the old walkist had something to look forward to amid all the tumbling sagebrush: Weston's tenth week on the road was in the books, and he had compiled another 219 miles, enabling him to set his sights on reaching Denver in the next week and the promise of a comfortable hotel, a meal, and company. A sign that Weston was getting close were some new walking companions, who joined him early in the week—not another hobo but a reporter from the *Denver Post* and four others. Assuming they could keep up with the seventy-year-old walkist, the conversation would be welcome.

The visiting pedestrians kept up for a while at least. Fortified by Sunday's rest, Weston, on Monday, May 24, trekked thirty-six miles without a stop from Hugo to Agate. All that to end up in a "town" with a store, a warehouse, and eight dwellings amid howling winds and persistent, soaking rain. By Tuesday the weather changed—to a driving hailstorm, in which Weston ambled a soggy twenty-five miles to Byers. "Getting my usual daily bath," the walkist quipped. Reading between the lines, you get the impression that Weston was stepping up the pace a tad but playing it cool to impress his presumably much younger walking comrades. It worked, and though the *Post* reporter had doggedly stuck with the pedestrian, he had suffered considerably in the rain. The other four, meanwhile, had ditched the walk and taken a train to Watkins, where they would rest and join Weston again for the triumphant walk into Denver.

The walkist anticipated reaching Denver by Tuesday evening; but the rains, the hail, and the need to walk along the rail bed were slowing the pace. Still not there on Wednesday, May 26, Weston hopped off the tracks and headed thirty-seven miles over slick, treacherous roads to Aurora. Now only seven miles south of Denver, he could have gotten there that night. But he felt it would be better to rest and head into Denver on Thursday, May 27, for a big daytime reception.

Weston was fortunate the *Post* reporter had stuck around.

A crowd of fifty were on hand to wish the walkist well as he pushed off from Aurora, with so many more along the road into Denver that the newspaperman was drafted to run interference and keep the path clear until the police could take over. By the time Weston crossed Denver's city limits, the streets were thick with fifteen thousand admirers. Weston basked in the attention but remained a man in a hurry. Governor John F. Shafroth was on the steps of the Capitol hoping to greet him; and though Weston raised his hat in greeting, he didn't stop. Doffing his cap and bowing to spectators on either side of the road, the pedestrian was deathly concerned that stopping or even slowing down in the crowd would cause someone to trample on his feet, as had happened two years before in Cleveland. "Keep away from my heels," he shouted again and again as he swung down Capitol Hill amid the scrum of people that threatened to engulf him. "If you injure a tendon there I am a goner."

The police did their job. Weston wasn't trampled, and on reaching his hotel, he decided to stay for the evening. The hoopla as much as the walking had tuckered him out. Besides, he wanted to see old friends, one of whom presented him with a golden inscribed seal ring. After spending the night in Denver, Weston was up and at it the following morning, accompanied by another friend from New York, Thomas Hogan, on the road north to Greeley. Hogan made it most of the way—stopping a mile short of the twenty-nine-mile journey to Greeley. Weston made it the whole way and spent the evening there after what was, for him, a short day. Then on Saturday, May 29, the old walkist headed another fifty-six miles to Cheyenne, Wyoming, despite some discomfort from breaking in a new pair of shoes.

What a week! Weston had covered 216 miles—a lot of hard going in his eleventh week. He sampled the gamut of Colorado's ecological wonderland, from the arid temperatures of eastern Colorado to the majestic wilderness of the Rockies. Remarkably durable, Weston felt strong, having dropped twenty pounds since mid-March, and now rounded out at a fit 135 pounds. The timing was apt. Some 2,614 miles into his trek across America, Weston was heading into week twelve needing every ounce of energy he could muster.

A week or so later, on Sunday, June 6, the *New York Times* ran a spread of photos of Weston in Denver. Among a handful of unstaged portraits of Weston's 1909 cross-country jaunt, the feature's three photos are revealing—most of all a portrait of Weston looking every bit of his seventy years. There he was with a brushy white mustache hanging well below his chin, a sombrero-sized sun hat perched at a raffish angle, and a grim, unsmiling demeanor—a cross between a desperado, Butch Cassidy, and Yosemite Sam. Next we see him trudging along the Union Pacific Railroad tracks accompanied by a delegation of ten. And next is another fascinating shot of Weston, giving an interview while slumped in a chair with his hands crossed, hat in lap, and feet thrown across another chair. To say that Weston looks tired in that last photo is an understatement; his whole body is slumped like a man in dire need of a long rest at the beach. He looks haggard, spent, whipped, and utterly exhausted, a polar opposite of the confident, stomach-thrusting walker peering from most of his studio shots.

Revealing as well is the headline, "Weston Passes Colorado and Enters on Hardest Stage of His Long Walk." That would be the uncompromising landscape of Wyoming, where the winds howled, the temperatures often plummeted, and towns were few and far between. Considering all of that was in store, the headline was spot on.

11

"Shut Up, You Jumping Jack!"

On November 14, 1885, Edward Payson Weston and Daniel O'Leary huddled in an office at 251 Broadway, just off City Hall Park in Manhattan. They were at the headquarters of *Turf, Field, and Farm* magazine—having undoubtedly walked part of the way to get there—to sign the articles of agreement for a 2,500-mile match race for a purse of $2,000 and two-thirds of the gate receipts offered by a New York temperance organization; the loser would take home $1,000 and the rest of the gate.

Both walkists looked to clear a marvelous payday—well over a year's salary—but they would have to work exceedingly hard for it. The old rivals would walk for twelve hours a day, except Sundays, at eastern and midwestern indoor liquor-free skating rinks and arenas and outdoors when the weather permitted. The prohibition angle wasn't as far-fetched as it sounds. The tour would be an extension of sorts of Weston's final days in Great Britain, from two years earlier when he had trekked those five thousand miles in one hundred days around England—averaging an astounding fifty miles a day, capping each evening with a lecture on the evils of alcohol. No wonder Weston always regarded the U.K. experience as his "star accomplishment."

In 1885 Weston was forty-six and O'Leary thirty-nine, both of them beyond their prime for the rigors of distance walking. The big-tent mania of competitive distance walking was on the wane anyway by then, given over in the United States to a growing interest in team sports like baseball and football. To underscore that walking's big days of mass six-day meets were a thing of the past, it had been less than a year since former champion Blower Brown had died in London at the age of forty-one. Few took note.

But Weston would concede nothing. He needed the income. And while people might have to strain their craniums to recall the glory days of Blower Brown, Weston's name still resonated. As stylish as ever, Weston showed up December 7 at Metropolitan Rink in Newark for his first race against O'Leary dressed in a close-buttoned winter sack coat, white tights, and light laced shoes—and he was as feisty as ever. "I haven't walked since March 1884 in England and then I covered five thousand miles," he told reporters. "O'Leary has always beaten me and he says he can again on a long trip. Now I don't think so. I propose to give his boast a practical test."

O'Leary looked like a man who was anxious to end the grueling race as quickly as possible. Surging to an immediate lead, O'Leary blazed through his first five miles in fifty-eight minutes and, day after day, tenaciously built the difference. Was Weston staying back by design, looking to snatch a late victory as he had in the 1879 Astley Belt? He wasn't saying. The atmosphere, meanwhile, was loads of fun, even surreal at times. At Metropolitan Rink in Newark, Weston and O'Leary circled a track that had been laid on the ice, thirteen laps to the mile, as skaters flew by and sometimes aped their styles, with walkists and skaters alike trying to stay in rhythm to the band. Two days later, Weston played his coronet while he walked, fought to take advantage of O'Leary's sore feet, and narrowed the gap to two miles. There, give or take a few hundred feet, O'Leary's lead would remain over the next few weeks as the pair moved on to New Brunswick and Plainfield, New Jersey; then to New

York, Syracuse, Rochester, Lockport, and Buffalo; Erie, Pennsylvania; Cincinnati; and finally Chicago.

Crowds varied. So did O'Leary's mood. On Christmas before a smattering of people at Cosmopolitan Skating Rink in New York, Weston launched into song in an effort to jump-start the holiday spirit. It's not recorded what the crowd thought, though it's likely that most got into the spirit. But not O'Leary. He was cracking. "Shut up, you jumping jack!" he shrieked across the rink at his opponent.

"I'll take my oath," answered Weston. "That man has no ear for Italian opera!"

That set the tone. The next day, Weston was limping and in clear discomfort; but energized by the crowd in his pocket and periodic bursts of speed, he felt confident. In the weeks that followed, O'Leary expanded his lead to as many as twenty-five miles but remained in a funk. On January 20 in Erie, the Irishman twice pushed Weston off the track, growing so unruly that the older walkist asked for police protection. Seeking the moral high ground but with a gleam in his eye, Weston addressed the audience, asking them to forgive O'Leary, who was said to be fighting illness. That got a rise from the crowd, who promptly cheered Weston while hissing O'Leary.

Most likely, O'Leary was ill and overwhelmed by the pressure, letting his more wily opponent get into his head. Then Weston began steadily chipping away at his opponent, picking up a mile here and there, one in Buffalo for instance and several more in Cleveland. By the time the two men left Cincinnati in late January for the grand finale in Chicago, Weston had narrowed the gap to nine miles. Though accounts of the rest of the competition are sketchy, O'Leary got drunk and collapsed on the track on February 2 in Chicago, according to one story. Two days later, he failed to show up. Weston did, however, and, passing both O'Leary and his 2,500th mile, became several thousand dollars richer for the effort. The great walkist had done it again by averaging forty-six and a quarter miles a day in fifty-four days of walking, feeling none the worse for wear: an hour later he was on the train headed home to New York.

. . .

"Walk out your troubles, or walk your troubles out of you," Edward Payson Weston counseled late in life. "There is no malady of mind or body that you can't walk away. Not one person in ten has exercised enough. Inaction gives you the blues and a poor stomach. The two together make bad nerves, bad tempers, and bad characters. Walking will cure all of these [maladies]. You don't get consumption or influenza or pneumonia or any of these epidemics that are flying around if you do ten miles a day."

Weston had ascribed to that philosophy for years. But his great 1885 match race against Daniel O'Leary would be his last competition. Two years later at forty-seven, Weston announced he was retiring from competitive walking. There the biographical trail goes a bit cold for the great walkist; his reasons for leaving the roads were unclear beyond a few infirmities and perhaps an ultimatum from his family. But just like that, there was Weston again, popping up in the mid-1890s to announce a return to distance trekking to combat his rheumatism, or so he said. Was Weston, who was already a restless soul, perhaps a tad bored and missing the limelight? Perhaps. "Walking," he explained, "defies all infirmities."

There is another reason Weston may have been anxious to return to competitive walking. If life on the road could be hard, it may have been preferable to being at home. Marriage for Weston and his wife, Maria, had never been easy, but in 1893 Ed left her. The final straw, according to their grandson Richard Litz, was an argument over the future of their son, Ellsworth, with whom Ed had a tense relationship. Weston ordered his son out of the house—perhaps not an outlandish demand given that Ellsworth was in his twenties—but Maria objected. That gave Edward Payson Weston "the excuse he needed," as his great-granddaughter Joyce wrote, and he was gone. "Their separation was no surprise to those who knew them," Joyce added. "It was simply the culmination of much marital strife, obvious to their children for a long time." Daughter Lillian agreed, describing the marriage as "the shackles they both hated."

It's likely that Weston also took to competitive walking again as a form of therapy, a stress reliever, and a way to earn some prize money. He continued paying the bills for three years until he approached Maria about a divorce so he could marry a twenty-something Irish immigrant, Anna O'Hagen—spelled as "Annie Hagan" in the 1910 U.S. Census and as "Annie O'Hagan" according to Litz. Variously described in news articles and gossip as Weston's niece, housekeeper, secretary, nurse, adopted daughter, and by wagging tongues as something significantly less dignified, O'Hagan was a blessing for Weston. She would be his companion for the rest of his days. In a thinly disguised unpublished short story titled "The Other Woman," Lillian described her mother's reaction: "I couldn't stop you from leaving," she told her husband, "but I'll never give you a divorce."

"So be it," Ed responded. "You'll never get another cent of support from me."

Lillian would never see her father again, keeping up with his exploits through the newspapers. After a successful career as a New York newspaper columnist, Lillian had met Frank Hazen by the early 1890s; they would marry and move to a ranch in Montana. The distance seemed to give her perspective. Though angry with Weston's behavior, Lillian still revered him; and instead of demonizing O'Hagan, Lillian remained grateful for her devotion to her father.

However, Maria would always be bitter. Talking years later

years with her mother, Lillian sought reason. "She didn't steal your husband," Lillian said of O'Hagan. "All this time she has lived with him and made him happy without sacred vows or legal bonds. I'll tell the world I take my hat off to her."

These were Victorian times, hard on the reputations of men and women who lived together but never married. Lillian recognized how much O'Hagan had given up to live with Weston. She had chosen to spend it with "a self-centered man," as Litz described him, "who always did as he pleased."

"They aren't even married—just living together unlawfully," Maria insisted to Lillian.

"And whose fault is that?" Lillian countered.

Years later, Lillian would write about the things she missed most about her father: "His enthusiasm, his hearty enjoyment of all the pleasures of life, his capacity for work or for entire relaxation when a task was done, and his old firm handshake and the twinkle of his eye."

Back on the roads, the old pedestrian may have lost a step or two but not his pluck or endurance. In December 1893 the fifty-four-year-old Weston, heeding the request of several physicians, tramped 160 miles north through the ice, mud, and snow from the Battery in Lower Manhattan to the State Capitol at Albany. Aiming to get there in seventy-two hours, he arrived in fifty-nine hours and fifty minutes. Weston had always been a medical marvel, noted by experts for his ability to cover long distances, but this was something else: a man in his midfifties who was defying the restrictions of age. An NFL quarterback still playing at forty is considered a marvel; so is a forty-five-year-old pitcher, even a knuckleballer. But here was Weston the Walkist still performing, admittedly a step or two slower than in the old days, well into his fifties. The legend was back to doing what he did best.

Weston had stopped walking against anyone but himself, pedestrianism's most notable solo practitioner. In 1896 he tried to replicate the feat of walking 112 miles inside twenty-four hours, from twenty-two years earlier. In front of society friends, industrialists, and New York City police commissioner Theodore Roosevelt, Weston broke down after 103 miles and tearfully declared, "I am a fool," and that "to fail breaks my heart."

Weston's spirits remained strong. A decade later, in 1906 at sixty-seven, he set out to walk from City Hall in Philadelphia to the Fifth Avenue Hotel in lower Manhattan in twenty-four hours. Stopping only once, for a thirty-minute nap in New Brunswick, Weston beat the deadline by six minutes. The next year, at age sixty-eight, he repeated an earlier journey from Portland to Chicago, beating his time from forty years before.

How could Weston be turning such marvelous feats in his late sixties? He wasn't just a freak of nature but first and foremost a remarkable physical specimen. He didn't smoke, drank sparingly, and watched his diet. As a walkist, he dressed for the weather, rested when necessary, and properly nursed any injuries. In the process, he had become a fitness visionary, a man who understood the importance of incorporating regular exercise at a time when many specialists and experts still did not.

Leave it to today's experts to demonstrate the wonder of Weston's extraordinary physical gifts as an older man. In a 1996 report, "The Age Antidote," Dr. Len Kravitz, program coordinator of exercise science and researcher at the University of New Mexico, argued that "improved health through physical activity has no finish line"—and in doing so, he states the clear connection of the persistent scientific association of exercise to better health in the elderly. Calling a sedentary lifestyle "a predisposition to disability, early death, and a depreciated quality of life," Dr. Kravitz pointed to a series of statistics that clearly demonstrate the physiological changes often triggered by aging. Those statistics ranged from a 20 to 30 percent decrease in cardiac output by age sixty-five for those with sedentary lifestyles to 30 percent decrease in strength, a 40 percent loss of muscle mass, and a 40 to 50 percent loss in forced vital lung capacity, all by the age seventy. "Educating the elderly to the positive aspects of including cardiovascular activity, muscle strength and flexibility in their life is a challenge for the health fitness professional," Dr. Kravitz argued. "Awareness must be directed to the fact that chronological age does not really represent quality of health."

But Weston wouldn't have been a good candidate for the study. He'd have skewed the statistics.

12

"That Awful Strain"

Both celebrated and cursed, the Wyoming winds howl because of a geographical quirk—the presence of the Continental Divide coupled with Wyoming's latitude relative to the warmer temperatures sweeping in from the Pacific Ocean.

Geography defines Wyoming. The Wind River Range, or "Winds" for short, is a prime spot for trout fishermen in western Wyoming. Just west of Laramie is the poetic-sounding Big Hollow Valley, the world's largest wind inversion depression, thought to have been formed from wind erosion. So intense do the winds blow in a rough triangle of land between Cheyenne, Laramie to the west, and Casper to the north that it has blown trains off tracks. East of Laramie is the Medicine Bow region, where in the 1970s Pittsburgh Plate Glass (PPG) Industries built two enormous wind turbines that were knocked over so many times that the company abandoned them. In recent years, growing demand for clean energy has made wind energy a big industry in Wyoming.

But the prospect of utilizing all that wind for energy was far in the future as Edward Payson Weston spent a restful Sunday, May 30, 1909, in Cheyenne and contemplated the next stage of his great journey across America. A century ago, wind was, well, just wind, forcing those who walked through it or farmed the soil it blew away to deal as best they could. In Weston's case, that meant the prospect of nearly two weeks of walking due west through this relentlessly harsh landscape.

Weston's very first steps into the state on Saturday had been a preview of sorts of not just the kind of conditions that awaited him in Wyoming but of how the weather could change in a flash. Leaving Greeley, Colorado, Weston called the conditions, "delightful." But suddenly around 10:00 a.m. a gale blew through just as the walkist headed through Colorado's Pawnee National Grassland, just south of the state line. Seemingly from nowhere, the winds blew and blew, and there wasn't much Weston could do. "Quite often I would get in the lee [air current] of a high mountain, which shielded me," he said of that long, hard day, "and again it would require all my strength to keep from being blown over . . . the wind had full play."

Weston had passed into the Rockies, some six thousand feet above sea level, where breathing could be labored. In the meantime, the towns were even more remote than anywhere back East. A case in point was the final ascent into Cheyenne, which Weston called, "the culmination of the most strenuous two weeks I have ever experienced in the whole course of forty-five years of walking." The old walkist often spoke in extremes after a particularly hard spell, but this time, he meant it. "The people east of Chicago have no idea of the force and magnitude of these elements of the West," he wrote. "Compared with the showers and breezes in the East they are awful and past comprehension. The showers come suddenly and in torrents and you are drenched to the skin." Weston set an ambitious schedule anyway for Wyoming, looking to average forty-seven miles a day along the southern railroad lines, roughly parallel to today's Interstate 80, through Laramie, Rawlins, Rock Springs, and Evanston into Utah. "I am . . . so used to having all sorts of obstacles piled up against me that I feel equal to any emergency."

Weston was half right. He *was* used to overcoming obstacles. But *forty-seven miles* a day through Wyoming? The prospect of difficult conditions confronted him from the get-go. On Monday, May 31, stormy conditions kept Weston in Cheyenne. On Tuesday, June 1, in a cold rain, he gritted nine miles by mid-morning over the mountains toward Laramie, to the 7xL Ranch (now Terry Bison Ranch), where he rested and took off again. It was rough slogging; and leaving the railroad bed for a time, Weston climbed over fences and through sheep pastures and cornfields before cutting his losses and hightailing it back to the ranch. Fortunately, it was a comfortable, spacious place to wait out the weather; owned by Wyoming's richest man, Senator Francis E. Warren, the ranch had hosted another restless traveler back in 1903: President Roosevelt.

Just past midnight on Wednesday, June 2, Weston finally caught a break. The storm had vanished, leaving a clear, brilliant sky and a shining moon—a real night walker's dream. Finally taking off for Laramie, Weston made his way serenaded by coyotes howling in the distance. Such a route in western New York or Pennsylvania would have taken him through small towns with ample opportunities for refreshment. But it was different in Wyoming, where cows and chickens were plentiful and there was no available milk or eggs—without which, he said, he felt lost. There was, however, plenty of snow, a reminder of the recent storms, as well as massive, steep mountains of solid rock and decomposed granite, all of which presented what Weston called "a wild, lonesome picture." There were even some people, mostly railroad section hands, who spoke Japanese, Italian, and Greek but little or no English and who almost certainly had no idea about the legend of Edward Payson Weston.

Weston soldiered onward anyway. By 7:30 p.m. on Wednesday, he was in Laramie, sixty miles closer to San Francisco. On Thursday, June 3, walking day number seventy, he made it forty miles to Rock River; and on Friday, June 4, and Saturday, June 5, another forty miles to Hanna, despite being blown thirty feet down an embankment. Every day came a new challenge. Heading from the mountains into the more barren Red Desert region of south-central Wyoming, Weston ate where he could, though the towns were sometimes twenty miles apart and most of the water was undrinkable. Who, if any, of the readers following his daily dispatches in the *New York Times* could relate to the kinds of challenges he faced? But the interest in Weston's epic walk was enormous, as was the concern that the seventy-year-old walkist was reaching the limits of his endurance.

Weston's 167 miles for the week was his weakest to date—and it was a turning point, putting his ultimate goal of reaching San Francisco in one hundred days in jeopardy. By doing the math, he could see his 2,747 miles in seventy-two days gave him twenty-eight days to cover the last 1,553 miles, requiring him to average a hefty 55 miles a day the rest of the way, with a lot of mountains and certain storms still ahead. Few doubted that he could reach San Francisco, but some began hinting that making it in one hundred days was nearly impossible. The chorus of doubters was led by his great admirers, the *Times*, which still allowed that since he made it most of the time, he could again. "The fact that Edward Payson Weston . . . has kept walking in the face of . . . a hurricane shows something more about his mental and physical condition than about the anemometric records recently made in the region through which is walking," the paper editorialized on June 8. "Theoretically, the hardest part of the route, with its combination of deserts and mountains, is still to be traversed, and as Weston is already behind his schedule to such an extent that, to win, each day's travel must be considerably longer than his previous average, success would seem to be impossible. He has the railroad to walk in, however, and luck and good weather, of which he has as yet had so little, might bring him to the coast within, or not far beyond, his early expectations."

. . .

Weston would be in Wyoming for another eleven days. Some were good, others were astoundingly hard. On Monday, June 7, while he was trekking forty miles from Hanna to Rawlins, a storm of biblical proportions pounded the region—hail followed by driving rain, which gobbled up railroad tracks and swept away bridges. The damage backed up trains by as much as fifteen hours and left Weston's manager, John Schinkel, far behind and unable to deliver adequate supplies and clothing. Five days later Weston was in Granger, still out of towels, which were with Schinkel, and sorely needing to replace his shoes.

Weston did get an extra pair of shoes, though from where he never said. Most likely, a trainman gave him a pair. By then, another challenge had emerged: hobos were everywhere, traveling the freights and scaring the old pedestrian, who had taken to packing a revolver for protection. Thank goodness then for Weston's guardian angels, several actually. They were Weston's many Union Pacific Railroad friends, who notified deputy sheriffs to pay particular attention to their walkist friend and would offer him first aid in Wasatch, Utah, where he fell and cut himself on a broken bottle. On June 16 those railroaders even set up a torch-holding escort for Weston through the railroad's one-and-a-half-mile Aspen Tunnel.

Back in New York, the *Times* editorial staff had a laugh about the liquid contents of that broken bottle. "Edward Payson Weston, in spite of storms and . . . wounds from a broken bottle—Edward P., by the way, is a total abstainer, so nobody need be suspicious about that bottle's contents . . . nearing his destination, if not at a rate within his allotted hundred days, at least at one marvelously rapid for a man of 70 years after walking three-quarters of the way across the American continent," it wrote June 19. "Most men of half his age would think that they had well earned a week's rest after achieving the distance traveled on any one of the days Weston calls bad," the paper continued. "His journey, though it may not end as soon as he hoped, will still have been an amazing display of human endurance and capacity. It does not now promise to be exactly a success, but it will be very far from a failure."

The *Times* had taken to illustrating Weston's dispatches with a small map pinpointing his progress, giving close-ups to obscure towns with poetic names like Church Butte and Castle Rock, Wyoming, and Echo Canyon, Utah. On June 17 Weston crossed into Utah, aware that he was following the railroad through the historic Mormon Pioneer Trail that Brigham Young and his followers had walked in the 1840s en route to Salt Lake City. Echo Canyon was one of the towns on the way, and so was Church Butte, a stunning sandstorm formation rising one thousand feet into the sky. Church members are said to have held services there during their journey; and John Boardman, an 1843 emigrant, described it as "a magnificent site" that was "of the shape of a large temple decorated with all kinds of images . . . gods and goddesses [and] animals."

Weston's immediate goal wasn't Salt Lake City but to the north at Ogden. It required a trek of 58 miles to get there on Saturday, June 19, his eighty-fourth day of walking, which would complete his fourteenth week at 3,101 miles. It had been a brutal week in which Weston had compiled only 149 miles, his shortest to date. But a day's rest and the promise of a few days of more plentiful lands before the Great Salt Lake Desert brought renewal, reflection, and a slight change of plans. From Ogden, Weston had planned to follow the San Pedro Railroad, which would have steered him southwest into Los Angeles. But after talking with the railroad men, he learned the towns along the way were often thirty miles apart—more distant than those spread-out towns in Wyoming. And so he switched to a new railroad—the Southern Pacific, which not only promised a more direct route but bigger towns along the way that weren't so far apart like Reno, Nevada, and the California towns of Niles, Redwood, and Sacramento. And this way Weston wouldn't have to go to Los Angeles and then head another 382 miles up the Pacific Coast to San Francisco. He would go directly to the Bay Area.

Officials of the Southern Pacific Railroad were delighted. Sensing all kinds of positive publicity in hosting the great Weston, they pledged immediate assistance the entire route to San Francisco. So starting Monday in Ogden, a refreshment-bearing railroad employee named Joseph Murray would accompany him the rest of the way on a velocipede, or speeder—the big-wheeled, gasoline-powered bicycle of the era. And railroad dining cars had been alerted to carry extra bags of ice for Weston's use should the train happen to pass the walking party.

The changes had immediate dividends. On Monday, June 21, Weston headed south out of Ogden and nearly halfway around the Great Salt Lake, some seventy-two miles to a spot west of Salt Lake City called Hogup. Heading another fifty-two miles due west through the Great Salt Lake Desert to Tacoma, Nevada, on Tuesday, Weston continued to feel strong, "all owing to strengthening food" provided by Joseph Murray, the man on the velocipede, Weston said. In the desert, it was hot, so hot that Weston rested the next two days between noon and 4:00 p.m. On top of that were sandstorms that clogged his nose and mouth with dirt. But Weston still felt better off than a week ago, filled with new perspective and thankful that he no longer was in godforsaken Wyoming. "Notwithstanding all this, conditions are so much better by reason of this new arrangement that I wonder how I ever stood that awful strain while walking through Wyoming."

In northern Nevada, Weston took to walking a good chunk of his daily distance in the cool of the evening. Leaving Tacoma at 7:45 a.m. on Wednesday and heading due west on a route roughly parallel to today's Interstate 80, he trekked twelve miles in three and a half hours to Noble and rested until the evening, when he headed another forty-one miles to Moor. But walking at night brought its own set of challenges. For starters, Wednesday had been moonless, making it impossibly dark and slow plodding. Night walking also cut into Weston's sleep, and when Weston awoke Thursday, he felt weary, so much so that he realized he had been overdoing it. So trekking all of nine miles Thursday to Wells, he decided to rest up until Friday. What a good decision it was; for back at it and feeling strong again Friday, Weston headed fifty-four miles all the way to Elko and another thirty-eight to Carlin on Saturday, June 27,—walking day number ninety. Though he was dropping more hopelessly behind schedule, Weston was his old upbeat self, compiling 252 miles in his fifteenth week of walking, his best week since Chicago. Weston didn't say he was disappointed that reaching the West Coast in one hundred days, after 3,353 miles, had become a mathematical impossibility. All he would say for the record was, "I shall make the best time possible in reaching San Francisco on July 9 at four o'clock." Chances are Weston didn't mind so much; he was feeling his old pep and nearing California.

. . .

The Southern Pacific Railroad Company hadn't so much entered a business arrangement with Weston as it adopted him. Two or three times a day, conductors dropped off bags of ice for the Weston party, as passengers whistled and called their regards from train windows. Mail for the pedestrian was tossed off the train as well; everyone connected with the railroad, it seemed, was connecting with Weston, with a letter, a telegram, or a simple wave of support. Late Thursday in the darkness near Wells, a gust of wind blew away Weston's hat. So much for the hat, he figured, until noon on Friday, when the conductor on a freight train spotted the hat at the bottom of a ravine in Friday's early daylight. The hat was retrieved, and railroad workers made sure that Weston soon had it back.

But even the good deeds shown to him by the trains offered no respite from the newest and perhaps the most bizarre challenge yet—the persistent Nevada mosquitoes. They were everywhere, thickening the sky in big black swarms easily seen from a distance in the arid, treeless, and virtually uninhabited prairie. "They came at me in bucketsful," Weston said. "I had heard much about the great Nevada desert and had been warned that it would be the most difficult part of my long walk, but this is not true. I did not mind the desert at all except when I ran into those mosquitoes and then I did suffer, but it was not the fault of the desert. I suffered from the bites of the mosquitoes."

If only Weston had carried repellent. Prowl the Internet, and you'll find several answers as to the origins of mosquito repellent. The first reported use of insect repellent dates to 425 BC, when Herodotus observed an Egyptian fisherman using oil extracted from the castor-oil plant, whereas the U.S. Army is said to have invented the modern repellent, the kind with the ingredient DEET, or diethyl-meta-toluamide, in 1946. Suffice it to say that Weston had neither castor oil nor DEET, leaving him virtually defenseless in contending with the pesky desert critters.

Anxious for relief and a break from the ninety-degree heat on Thursday, July 1, at Iron Point, Weston ducked into the only available shelter he could find, the rear of a tollhouse. But the mosquitoes were everywhere, forcing Weston to build a fire in hopes of smoking out the pesky insects. "The Nevada mosquito is not so easily defeated, and [with the fire], I finally escaped, being badly stung and sore," he said. His other defense was the cool, mosquitoless desert nights, of which Weston took full advantage, covering as much distance as possible in the dark. By doing so, he made steady progress—fifty miles on July 1 to Humboldt; twenty-eight miles on July 2 to Mill City, where it hit 114 degrees in the shade; and fifty-seven miles on July 5 through the Humboldt Range of western Nevada to

Hazen. A long day's journey short of Reno, on the morning of July 6, Weston grabbed a few hours of extra sleep, wanting to be sharp because town officials were planning a big welcome. After the wilds of Wyoming and all those pesky Nevada mosquitoes, Weston could hardly wait.

. . .

Reno, Nevada, in 1909 was a small town with big ambitions, looking to make its name as a major sporting venue. Its breakthrough would come a year later, on Independence Day 1910, when the city of seventeen thousand demonstrated it was easily accessible and could throw a party. Reno hosted a big-time heavyweight title fight that day in which the champion Jack Johnson retained his belt by stopping the former champion, Jim Jeffries, in a fifteenth-round technical knockout.

Some thirty thousand people squeezed into Reno for the event, thanks largely to the Southern Pacific, which for days had been operating special trains from San Francisco. By fight day Reno was a "swirling, seething maelstrom of rushing, crushing, colliding bodies," as one called it. Streets were jammed, and the hotel lobbies were "packed to suffocation," the observer said; and patrons, "once crushed in through the doorways, [found] it impossible to move hand or foot." In the meantime, thousands clamored for rooms, with many sleeping wherever they could, from park benches to hammocks and even billiard tables. "The lobbies of hotels were lined with cots; so were their flat graveled roofs," the observer said. Thousands of locals rented out spare rooms in their homes. And somehow, statistics were compiled, with an estimated 5,375 sleeping on the banks of the Truckee River, 4,425 on the grass of the public park, 125 in funeral parlors, and 17 bedding down in the city morgue. Just how those numbers were actually acquired isn't recorded.

Clearly, Reno had a ways to go in 1910 in becoming a sports

mecca. Throwing open the welcome mat for Edward Payson Weston in 1909 was simpler, a dress rehearsal of sorts for the following year's big bout. The old pedestrian had been expected in town at some point in the early evening of Wednesday, July 6; when it became apparent he was late in completing the forty-six-mile trek from Humboldt, expectant residents of Reno went to him. Marching some five miles east to a point in the road halfway to Sparks, some two hundred townsmen met Weston and, despite the hour, accompanied him the rest of the way into Reno. Mayor A. M. Britt was disappointed; he had waited three hours in the office of the *Nevada State Journal*, hoping to greet Weston as part of a parade. But when Weston still hadn't appeared by midnight, he gave up and went home, as did the members of the Reno City Band.

Finally striding into Reno at 2:00 a.m., Wednesday, July 7, Weston met up with Schinkel as he headed straight to the Golden Hotel, with a few quick thank-yous here and there before going to bed. Mayor Britt never got his ceremony, but no one seemed any worse for wear. Weston stopping in Reno was still a very big deal, filling the newspapers with front-page news. It marked the beginning of the end to the great walk; with only 244 miles to go, Weston was headed to mountainous but bountiful country after ninety-eight days of walking. The home stretch was just ahead—and after a restful evening, the old walkist was filled with good cheer and willing to overlook the prospect of not reaching San Francisco in one hundred days. "I am a few days behind time but that is not my fault," he reasoned the next day in an interview with the *Reno Evening Gazette*. "It is because I followed the road [most] of the way. In taking this great walk again, I would not follow the railroad as I find . . . I cannot walk more than three miles an hour when four miles an hour should be my average."

There was another reason Weston was feeling so upbeat. Schinkel and Murray were both on schedule and ably doing their jobs. So was the newest member of the traveling support team, a member of the Southern Pacific engineering staff named C. Elmer Brown, who had just arrived from Sacramento and would accompany the traveling party through the steepness and treachery of the Sierra Mountains. Fortified by a heap of knowledge about the local terrain, Brown would be invaluable in guiding Weston in the final miles of his great American trek.

Weston was feeling chatty during his few hours of rest Wednesday, July 7, in Reno. "What was your diet in the desert?" a reporter asked him. On a walk, he rarely touched meat, the great man said. For breakfast, he had taken to dining on two poached eggs, porridge, and three cups of coffee. Lunch was lighter and often just milk when available. Dinner was problematic in the desert, sending Weston to the cart for milk, eggs, rice pudding, and soft drinks. In the meantime, the pedestrian was already thinking of life after San Francisco, having already received a $30,000 offer to lecture for twenty weeks and another offer from a vaudeville house. But for now, "I am not walking on a wager, and I am not being paid by any newspaper," Weston reminded his audience. "In fact, I am walking just to prove that I can walk four thousand miles in one hundred days."

The only sour note of the entire day was Weston's raw recollections of his serial difficulties in Wyoming. As a master self-promoter, he was almost always upbeat about most any region he had visited—a walking, talking travel bureau for just everywhere except Wyoming. "I pray to be protected from Wyoming," he said. "It is the worst state in the United States. They have no milk, eggs, or other nourishing food there, and the roads are fearful. . . . Oh, it was fierce in that state, and if I ever walk across the continent again, I will surely cut [it] out."

Weston rested most of the day in his fourth-floor room at the Golden Hotel, planning to take off for California and points west at 6:00 p.m. to reach San Francisco in six days. Locals swarmed the lobby in hopes of catching a glimpse of him, with all eyes on the elevator, hoping the next person to appear would be the man of the hour himself. Though there is no record of how many of those people met Weston and accompanied him out of Reno, it was probably a swarm. The old walkist himself reported that the city "gave me a great send-off."

Ahead loomed the lush, soaring majesty of the Sierra Mountains. Weston and his party would be walking just north of Lake Tahoe, where the Southern Pacific Railroad wound through narrow canyons along the Truckee River. The stunning panorama thrilled Weston, as did cooler temperatures, which offered a reviving and welcome relief after the desert and those swarms of mosquitoes. "The air is chilly, though bracing and the walking is excellent," the walkist gushed. "I never felt so well and hearty in my life."

Weston passed into California, the final state of his walk across America, at 4:58 a.m. A few miles later he sauntered into Truckee, where Brown was waiting and set to accompany him through the Sierras. Brown's guidance was a godsend. The traveling party would spent much of the following two days and nights, maneuvering by a mind-numbing forty-one miles of snow sheds and gingerly moving ahead in the dark along narrow, treacherous paths by lantern, where only a slip or a false step could send them hundreds of feet to a certain death. So cramped was the space along the railroad path that every half hour when a train whistled past, the walking crew had to foist themselves erect between the sheds. To "realize that it was less than twelve inches from your breast, while the terrific puffing of two immense engines nearly deafening you is certainly enough to make one nervous," Weston said.

. . .

It could have been the altitude. Or perhaps it was just a bout of loneliness during some downtime, when Weston often grew reflective about his reasons and rationale for making his great walk. Whatever the reason, Weston was distraught and emotional on Sunday, July 11, 1909, in Rosemont, which was likely to be his last day of rest before reaching San Francisco.

"If anyone had told me six months ago that I would undertake to walk over railroad tracks between Chicago and San Francisco for 2,577 miles, and practically without attendants or necessary refreshments for 1,800 miles of that distance, I would have said, 'I am not such an idiot,'" Weston said. "I am not saying this to excuse this wretched failure. I am simply stating facts. . . . This has been an effort which should be called one chapter of mistakes from beginning to end. . . . This is the most crushing failure I have [encountered] in my career."

Weston had realized some days ago that he wouldn't be getting to San Francisco in one hundred days. But it hadn't bothered him until now, an off day with the time to think. Out streamed a torrent of pent-up disappointment and anger about time-wasting decisions in one part of the trip or another that had delayed him. Weston said he should never have relied on "a miserable and worthless automobile" in the East. Railroad walking in the West had slowed him as well, and a trainman told Weston he had probably added another two hundred miles to his trip by having to walk diagonally at times up the tracks. And though Weston didn't say it then, it had to have dawned on him that a more direct route in the East and Midwest would have saved a bunch of miles and sliced into the time. Adding to those fatal decisions, Weston admitted he should have traveled east instead of west to avoid facing a lot of the weather head-on, which common wisdom said went the other way. "I should have gone from San Francisco to New York," he cried. "Then the tornadoes, gales, and drenching rains invariably coming from the West would have driven me into New York instead of depriving me the use of the road for fifteen days out of the one hundred."

On the surface, Weston's seventeenth and last full week of walking had been among his best. From Reno, he had steadily trekked through the mountains 68 miles Wednesday, July 8, to Cisco on day one hundred of his trip, followed by 38 miles on Friday, July 9, to Colfax, and another 36 miles on Saturday, July 10, to Roseville, just northeast of Sacramento—240 miles for the week. But the week had been emotional, and the strain of trudging all those laborious miles past the snow sheds along narrow rail lines had taken a toll. So had the gnawing realization that if not for all those gales, tornadoes, and other factors, he would have easily reached San Francisco in one hundred days, instead of being several days and 144 miles short of the end. "With all this," Weston added, "I am in the best of health, but much depressed in spirits."

His comments drew headlines. "Weston Laments His Many Mistakes," trumpeted the headline in the *Times* on Monday, July 12. But early that morning, Weston already had moved on. An emotional man, he was used to getting things out quickly and leaving behind whatever was on his mind. At issue for the moment was how he would actually finish his great walk, because his last day required two ferry rides, including the three-mile ride from Oakland across the Bay to San Francisco. To compensate for the distance, Weston planned on walking an extra six miles—three for each ride. As Weston noted slyly, "I could not walk over the Bay." Not only was Weston nearly finished; his wit was back.

Three days remained in Weston's great trek across America. The first two passed uneventfully. Heading through Sacramento on Monday, July 12, Weston covered thirty-nine miles to Dixon in punishing 110-degree temperatures; he then added another thirty-seven miles on Tuesday to a spot just north of Oakland across Suisen Bay near Vallejo. On Wednesday, July 14, his 105th day of walking, Weston rose before dawn and headed due south. Accompanying him were Schinkel, Murray, and Brown, his hearty support staff of three who the old walkist may have wished had been there for him from the get-go.

Others had shown up as well, namely several newspapermen set to record Weston's every ache, pain, and tidbit of philosophy in what was projected as the last day of his great American walk. Starting slowly, the pedestrian worked out the usual stiffness but soon "got into his lively stride," despite high winds that snuffed out the light in his lantern, noted an accompanying *New York Times* correspondent. Careful to retrace his steps for three miles to cover the distance riding the ferry from Benicia at Carquinez Strait to Port Costa, Weston headed steadily toward San Francisco, reaching Crockett, some thirty miles from the finish, at 11:30 a.m. and Pinole, six miles closer to the end, at 1:50 p.m.

By 8:00 p.m. Weston was in Oakland at the end of the line of the Southern Pacific Railroad Company, where a contingent of railroad officials and workers greeted him. "This company did so much for me that I fail to find words to express my appreciation," the grateful pedestrian told them. Then Weston retraced his steps for three miles to compensate for the second and final ferry ride—across the Bay—and hopped aboard the 10:18 boat to San Francisco. Offered a seat, Weston politely declined. While wading through a stack of letters and congratulatory telegraphs, he preferred standing.

Within the hour, Weston was in San Francisco, finishing his great walk across America the instant he stepped off the ferry onto the dock, some thirty-two miles for the day. He was at the end, finally, having trekked 3,898 miles from the Post Office in New York and clear across the continent in 105 days. In doing so, he had headed through snow, wind, drenching rain, gale-force winds, and tornados. He had conquered the heat and the altitude along with mud, nasty dogs, mosquitoes, supply mishaps, menacing hobos, inedible food, and sometimes no food at all. At different times along the way, Weston had injured his arm, foot, and ankle. In addition to walking, he had crawled at times and gone over and under fences and through fields. For every big city Weston had visited on the way, he had passed through a hundred small towns and villages, where his presence was one of the biggest events in years. At seventy years old, he had averaged a shade under thirty-eight miles a day, often leaving behind his decades-younger companions and walking, on average, six days a week. It was an epic feat of athletic endurance, one of the greatest ever.

"[This] was a great walk, and but for unforeseen difficulties and hardships in the last three weeks on my journey, I would have been here on the one hundredth day," Weston said. "Still, I am fine and could do it over again." Given what he had just accomplished, you would think the old pedestrian would have come up with something more inspiring, but such is the way of some great athletes for whom there is nothing short of perfection. In 1980, after the Pittsburgh Steelers had taken its fourth Super Bowl in six years, a television commentator asked the team's middle linebacker Jack Lambert for his reaction. The softball question was designed to draw a grateful smile, a bead of emotion, and thanks all round. But not this time—bearing his game face topped by a Pittsburgh Police baseball hat, the scowling Lambert was upset that the heavily favored Steelers had needed to rally from behind for the win. So it was with Weston, finished but unsatisfied. In his mind, he should done better.

Weston left the poetry to others, none of whom cared a fig that Weston hadn't crossed America in his self-imposed, hundred-day deadline. "San Francisco is not Seattle, of course, nor is 105 days 100," the *Times* wrote in an editorial, "but when a man in his 71st year walks from New York even to the nearer of the two cities and in the longer of the two times, the difference between purpose and achievement constitutes only a technical failure, and Edward Payson Weston can console himself with the thought that he is the object of about as much wonder as he would have been had he reached his originally chosen destination on the date fixed by his hopes."

That was spot on. "That he did not do so seems to have been due in no degree to a diminution of his pedestrian powers as a result of age," the paper continued. "On the contrary, he reached the coast in a condition apparently as good as that he was in when he started, and his delays were caused by obstacles— storms, excessive heat, failure of supplies and the like—that were unforeseen accidents of the journey, and would have kept back a younger man, or Weston himself in his prime, to the same extent."

No one disagreed. However, there was considerable debate whether Weston could have reached San Francisco in one hundred days using a more direct route. In a July 18 letter in the *Times*, Robert Bruce, editor of *The Official Automobile Blue Book*, wrote that Weston could have shortened his transcontinental walk in several places. Bruce points out that taking the Chicago and Northwestern direct route from Chicago through Des Moines and Omaha to Cheyenne, instead of detouring south to St. Louis and then west, would have cut a whopping five hundred to six hundred miles, surmising "it is difficult to see why he should have chosen . . . the route [he did]." In New York State, Weston tacked on mileage, Bruce added, by turning west and then north-northwest at Troy, instead of heading south-southwest several miles south at Albany. Later, Weston put on another seventy-five to one hundred miles by heading southeast from Buffalo to Olean instead of hugging Lake Erie and walking westward toward Ohio. Most likely, Weston headed out of his ways to lecture. "In brief, the transcontinental record can easily be put considerably under 100 days, if Mr. Weston ever desires to make a scientific study of his route," Bruce added. "In case he ever tries for a better record he can easily obtain accurate data that will prove of immense benefit to him."

On Thursday, July 15, Weston slept late, breakfasted, and seemed in no hurry to complete the last task of his journey—delivering the letter to San Francisco postmaster Arthur Fiske from his New York postmaster counterpart, Edward Morgan. Dated March 15, 1909, the letter had been carried by Weston for the entire trip. "It is a big undertaking for a man of Mr. Weston's years or for any man," Morgan had written in the letter. "But he is not made of the stuff that fails, and from what I know of his past performances, I am sure he will make good." Leaving his hotel in the early afternoon, Weston made a final walk by sauntering the half mile or so to the post office, saluted by many in the lunchtime crowd along the way. Fiske was waiting for him; and with the letter handed over, the greatest walk in American history was history.

"Meanwhile," said Weston, already thinking ahead, "the only trouble I have is an awful appetite."

. . .

It's likely that Weston ate well and often in those first few days after completing his task. Lingering in San Francisco, he waded through hundreds of congratulatory letters and telegrams, along with several offers to lecture. Having incurred $2,500 in expenses for the trek, Weston mulled over the opportunities, while looking to pay off his creditors and "striving to elevate in popular esteem the exercise of walking." Still bothered by not meeting his hundred-day deadline, he considered for a time turning right around and walking back to New York. Eventually, he would walk that way by incorporating a more direct route from Los Angeles to New York—but not right away. For now, Weston decided to take a train back to New York; not only were his backers dead set against an immediate walking trip home, but the pedestrian had sorted through the batch of offers and decided to appear in a few select places.

So several days later at the thirty-ninth-annual Steuben

County Old Settlers' meeting in Angola, Indiana, near Fort Wayne, there was Weston hopping off the eastbound train from Chicago and, according to a snarky reporter, giving "a demonstration of his easy walking in going from the hotel to the park." Arriving home in New York on August 16, he again expressed disappointment at not meeting his hundred-day goal, but he had also come to some important decisions: Weston said he would attempt the transcontinental walk again in early 1910, sticking to a shorter, more direct west-to-east route, while making arrangements well ahead of time for railroad employees to lend a hand. This time, Weston would stick to walking without lecturing, which took him off the route and sapped energy. And traveling through the West in mid-to-late winter would guarantee cooler temperatures.

Weston was true to his word. At 4:00 p.m. on February 1, 1910, he pushed off from Los Angeles for New York in a walk projected to be 3,500 miles—some 400 miles shorter than the one in 1909. And he vowed to get there not in one hundred walking days but in ninety—hoping to greet New York mayor William J. Gaynor on the steps of City Hall by May 17. In the West, at least, his route was different, a more southerly and direct route than in 1909, taking him to Chicago along the tracks of the Atchison, Topeka, and Santa Fe Railroad. Accompanying him was a car stocked with provisions, and railroad employees were on the lookout to supply food and shelter as needed. There would be problems—outside Kingman, Arizona, Weston slipped and banged his knee—but for most of the way, he felt good, enjoying generally decent weather and making better time than he had expected. On March 15, to honor Weston on his seventy-first birthday, a crowd of one thousand in Kinsley, Kansas, presented him with a gold watch as the old pedestrian reached town having just walked seventy-two miles. Four days later, Weston was in Elmdale, Kansas, and pronounced himself, "strong as a lion, except for a small strain in my right side."

From Chicago, Weston shifted from the rails back to public roads and endured the usual early spring ice and mud calamities. That slowed Weston a little, as did swallowing some tainted clam broth—"the hoodoo," he called it—in Syracuse; but the old pedestrian continued to stay on track. "I started out on a schedule to tramp the 3,500-odd miles in ninety days," Weston said in Yonkers, within a day's shot of the end. "I knew in my own heart—and I frequently told my friends so—that I should beat that time by more than ten days. Well, without being too egotistical about it, I've given that schedule a good licking, haven't I?"

And so on May 2—day seventy-five, a remarkable fifteen days ahead of his goal—there he was bounding up the steps of New York City Hall amid an adoring crowd in the tens of thousands, to vigorously pump the mayor's hand. Turning to Mayor Gaynor at City Hall, Weston called himself "a young old man of seventy-one years," adding that he "found that the nation excels not only in strong men but beautiful women."

"I wanted to show them all what I could do," he added, "and I'll bet I've made them all sit up and take notice."

So he had. By crossing the country in seventy-five days, Weston averaged a shade above forty-six miles a day—considerably better than the thirty-eight he had averaged the year before—and drawn the usual superlatives. "To drive a good horse 40 miles a day for so many consecutive days would be accounted cruelty to a dumb beast," the *Times* wrote in an editorial. "It needs all a strong man's courage, determination, comprehension of his powers and limitations to keep such a task. . . . Weston has again shown the endurance at which a human being of no extraordinary muscular development may be capable of late in life." Some days later, Weston's friend Walter Moler threw him a dinner that included a testimonial booklet, *Weston and his Walks*, which inside featured a day-by-day synopsis of this latest walk, calling it "the crowning effort of his professional career."

On the surface, it looked like that. A seventy-one-year-old man had set a goal to walk across America in ninety days and got there in seventy-five. It was astounding. But arguably, Weston's 1909 trek was the greater of the two walks—not only longer but filled with more—more extreme weather, more mud, more broken-down cars, and more challenges around every bend in the road. No wonder the 1909 walk "attract[ed] more attention than the other [walks]," the *Oakland Tribune* wrote some years later, "until wherever men spoke of Weston they thought of walking and an old man who found it good." There was also more learning in Weston's 1909 walk, on which he learned the importance of partnering with the rail companies in order to walk the tracks and establish supply routes. It was then that he reaffirmed the importance of achieving balance and of having a car that worked. All of these were substantial steps that ensured Weston's later success.

How best then to compare the two walks? Look at the 1909 photo of Weston's broken and discarded shoes, the soles badly worn. That was what it was like to walk across the country in 1909 against impediments that would have felled a lesser man. And that's why the 1909 walk by Edward Payson Weston, a superstar of his day and a man who had inspired a generation to get out and exercise, is among history's most underappreciated sporting achievements.

Epilogue

"I've Taken My Last Walk"

"It was a great walk all right, and I'm glad that it has ended as happily as it has," said Edward Payson Weston in Yonkers, just north of New York City, as he was about to complete his great 1910 tramp across America. "It's good to be back. . . . I've taken my last walk. It's up to the young men now. . . . Never again."

Not that anyone really believed him. Weston was slowing down, but he didn't head softly in the night. Not he. New York City's official subway had opened only six years before and was revolutionizing travel around Manhattan, but Weston still preferred to walk. How foolish, he argued, it was to ride from Times Square to City Hall unless you were in a terrific rush. Subways and elevated lines, and surface cars for that matter, were for old women and children in arms, he added, not for him. And so Weston kept walking because it was what he did.

In 1913 the seventy-five-year-old pedestrian spent two months trekking 1,546 miles from New York to Minneapolis, where he laid the cornerstone for the new clubhouse at the Minneapolis Athletic Club. Enamored by the beauty of the region and forever restless, Weston announced a few weeks later that he had bought a property five miles from Warroad in the Lake of the Woods region of northern Minnesota and that he would become a farmer there. Little more was said about that; instead, Weston returned to New York, where his name cropped up periodically in the news, particularly on his birthday, when he was always good for a quote.

In 1922 the eighty-four-year-old Weston took another walk, which would turn out to be his last really long one—setting out to tramp from Buffalo to New York City, some 450 miles, in thirty days. He made it in twenty-eight, beating his goal by two days and averaging sixteen miles a day. After spending his last night on October 6 at the Hotel Theresa in Harlem, Weston made the final, triumphant leg of his journey down Broadway to City Hall. It was just like old times, except that poor Mayor Gaynor had been shot and killed by a discharged city employee. But the new mayor, John Hylan, rose to the occasion, giving Weston a rousing welcome with all the trappings.

By then Weston and Annie O'Hagan had moved to a farm, not in the wilds of northern Minnesota, but one considerably closer to New York City. Their new residence was approximately ninety-five miles north of Manhattan near New Paltz, where Weston and Miss Anna, as she was known in town, had actually become a threesome. The newest family member was an orphaned boy from across the road named Raymond Donaldson, whose parents had perished in the flu epidemic of 1918. For the most part, life was quiet, and neighbor Louis Yess recalled years later, to journalist Vivian Yess Wadlin, how his father had periodically given a hand to the old pedestrian's family by hitching up Weston's horse to his surrey and driving it to the train station at Highland Landing to meet Weston and Miss Anna and take them home. Another time, Weston went to the Yess farm to ask for Mr. Yess's help in putting down a disabled horse. Apparently, Weston owned a small-caliber rifle that was unable to do the deed. So Yess did the job for him, as Weston, the king of roads on two continents, stood by and cried "like a baby."

Weston could have used the rifle on May 15, 1924, when the eighty-six-year-old pedestrian was beaten and shot in the leg in an odd burst of violence—a gang attack at his family's farm. No one else was injured in the attack, which news reports said may have involved several lawless locals notorious for storming abandoned farms to strip and sell the wood. Seemingly overwhelmed, the old pedestrian fought his attackers anyway and wound up in the hospital, where he was said to recover quickly. But did he? After that unfortunate attack, Weston headed into a long, steady decline.

Three days later Weston announced plans to leave the region and hit the trail again, hoping to walk forty miles in twenty-four hours—about one-third the distance he had walked forty years ago in his prime. However, Weston's only trail from that point was the restless pursuit of another place to live. He, O'Hagan, and young Donaldson first left the farm and moved to Fischer's Hotel in nearby Kingston. By 1927 they were in Philadelphia, then back in New York City, living in a tiny flat at 238 West Thirteenth Street, where the old pedestrian's health headed into free fall.

In 1926 Weston was found disoriented and rambling the streets of Manhattan. Taken to the Bellevue Hospital, he was diagnosed with "senile psychosis." Less than a year later, in June 1927, at eighty-eight, Weston seemed to have retained much of his old enthusiasm, though he was bedridden and dependent on O'Hagan who said she was having "a lively time" trying to stay out of poverty. Tracked down by a newspaper reporter, the old pedestrian talked about boxing and the stunning accomplishment the previous year of New Yorker Gertrude Ederle in swimming the English Channel in record time. And he desperately needed work—a messenger job, just like old times, if possible. The alternative, he said, was starving.

No jobs panned out. But on the day of the newspaper article, which included the old pedestrian's address, an eighty-year-old Civil War veteran knocked on Weston's door and peeled off a thirty-five-dollar donation. The fellow veteran didn't volunteer his name but contributed, he said, out of admiration for the great walkist's accomplishments; sixty-six years before, he had been in Washington DC when Weston strode in for President Lincoln's inauguration. Nor was he the only benefactor. Within days, Fernand Bardiani of West Seventy-Second Street, a self-described "middle-aged brother athlete," contributed ten dollars, and Mary B. Cleveland of the Town Hall Club delivered soup and sandwiches. They were among a handful of admirers who passed along another thirty-one dollars in contributions. A book publisher, Berkeley Press, even offered the old pedestrian a job carrying proofs about town; but O'Hagan, concerned that Weston would not be able to remember directions, turned it down.

Enter Anne Nichols, a thirty-six-year-old playwright and producer, and her manager, William de Lignemare, who, unlike Weston, were on a hot streak. Nichols's comedy *Abie's Irish Rose*, which depicted the tumult that arises with the marriage of a young Jewish man to an Irish woman, had debuted to poor reviews on Broadway back in 1922 but turned into a commercial tour de force anyway. The *Cats* of its day, Nichols's play would close that October after 2,327 performances, making it the longest-running play in Broadway theater history at the time. Though Nichols had just left for Europe to supervise production of her play there, she had decided to set aside $30,000 for the old pedestrian's maintenance and care. Under the terms, Weston would receive monthly installments of $150, to be administered by the Catholic Big Sisters, for the rest of his life.

The gift was pegged as an eighty-eighth-birthday present. Nichols was still away on March 16, 1927, when the New York Press Club threw in their own gift, a smaller fifty-dollar check and a celebratory luncheon. Members gave Weston a large silver cup and a cake with eighty-eight candles; afterward, the party repaired to City Hall, where the old pedestrian made friends with another mayor of New York City, the dapper Jimmy Walker. "I've met every mayor of New York City since I was a police reporter," the old pedestrian said. And with that, he invited the mayor to accompany him in the summer to a baseball game at Yankee Stadium. Delighted, Walker accepted.

Weston never got there. A week later, while crossing the street with Raymond Donaldson on the way to church to give thanks for Nichols's bounty, the man who made it through every danger on roads from New York to California—from tornados to sandstorms, deep snow to searing heat, hobos to angry gamblers—was struck by a cab and seriously injured. Taken to St. Vincent's Hospital in Manhattan, Weston was treated for a fractured skull and cuts. The injury was debilitating. Weston the Walkist was confined to a wheelchair and would hardly walk again.

On March 15, 1929, Edward Payson Weston quietly celebrated his ninetieth birthday. Having moved to 205 Taaffe Place in the Clinton Hill section of Brooklyn, he, O'Hagan, and Donaldson invited the neighbors to enjoy with them a cake topped with ninety blue, pink, and yellow candles. It was Weston's last public appearance; for on May 13, 1929, he died at home. O'Hagan and Donaldson were with him. But his wife Maria; his daughter Maud Beard and her two children, Ruth and Margaret; and his other daughter, Lillian Hazen, who had moved to Lewistown, Montana, and her son, Richard, had all stayed away.

Two days later, Weston was buried at St. John Cemetery in Middle Village, Queens, a Roman Catholic burial ground where, in future years, a cross section of New York's famous and infamous would be interred, from the pedestrian's old friend Mayor Hyland to strongman Charles Atlas, Congresswoman Geraldine Ferraro to crime figures including Lucky Luciano and John Gotti. The death of America's greatest ambulator—a man who thought nothing of walking forty to fifty miles a day (day after day after day) and among the most courageous, inspirational, quotable, occasionally irascible, and admired sportsmen of his day—prompted a new round of awe and remembrances. "Today, most men use their feet to press upon accelerators and do their walking upon the golf links," the *Oakland Tribune* wrote. "Cross country 'hikers' signal for lifts and so make the distance in a few days. But if one goes back in the foothills and mountains, or takes the trails in the forests, he will find members of the Weston club, some of them rugged old boys, as he was, stepping off the miles at seventy and more."

Putting more of a metaphysical spin on his passing, the *New York Times* wrote that Weston "had been of more cheer and help to others along the way of life than he could have ever known, even with all the applause, along the way."

"He has gone at last on what one has called 'the perfect walk,' the walk for which solitude is essential," the paper continued. "But in his pilgrimage across the Earth he has also led a multitude who will keep on walking till they, too, come to the end of the road which is the longer for going on foot."

NOTES

Prologue

vii **"Here he comes!":** "Weston Lectures after Long Walk," *New York Times*, March 23, 1909; "On Foot from New York to San Francisco," *New York Times*, March 28, 1909; "Edward Payson Weston the Guest of Syracuse," *Syracuse Herald*, March 23, 1909; "Is a Grand Old Man," *Syracuse Herald*, March 28, 1909.

x–xi **"Weston's name [became] a household word":** Litz, *Montana Frontier*, 5.

xii **Covering fifty miles in ten hours:** Marshall, *King of the Peds*, 35–40.

xii **"the greatest recorded labor":** O'Hagan, "There Was Nothing Pedestrian about One Edward P Weston."

xiii **"I never was a fast walker":** Litz, *Montana Frontier*, 5, 6.

xiii **Observers admired his unorthodox style:** Quotations gathered at Walkapedia.org, "Weston Walking Style and Technique," *Walking: The World on Foot and Online*, last modified December 4, 2009, http://walkapedia.org/walking/reading/research/137-weston-walking -style-a-technique.html.

xiii **"You'll see a little man":** Long, "On the Road with Weston."

xiii **"It seemed as though":** Long, "On the Road with Weston."

xiv **"Moving freely and gracefully":** "On Foot from New York to San Francisco," *New York Times*, March 28, 1909.

xv **"The fact was":** Litz, *Montana Frontier*, 6.

xv **"I feel much encouraged":** Litz, *Montana Frontier*, 6.

xvi **"The condition of the whole man":** Litz, *Montana Frontier*, 7.

xvi **"I ask for pardon":** "On Foot from New York to San Francisco," *New York Times*, March 28, 1909.

xix **"the generous hospitality of the people":** "Weston Plods Along, Finds Better Roads," *New York Times*, March 18, 1909.

xix   **"Say," he mused:** "On Foot from New York to San Francisco," *New York Times*, March 28, 1909.

1. "Worried about the Outcome of This One"

1   **The main door of the General Post Office:** "Weston at 71 Starts 4,300-Mile Walk," *New York Times*, March 16, 1909; "Weston's Walk across the Continent," *New York Times*, June 20, 1909.

4   **Edward Payson Weston's meandering route:** "Big Pedestrian Events Being Planned by Young and Weston," *New York Times*, February 28, 1909; "Weston at 71 Starts 4,300-Mile Walk," March 16, 1909; New York Times; "Weston's First Stop at the Yonkers Y.M.C.A. on His New York-Frisco Walk," *Yonkers Herald*, March 16, 1909; "Weston, Walker and Talker," *Yonkers Statesman*, March 16, 1909.

6   **It was 9:15 p.m.:** "Weston, Walker and Talker," *Yonkers Statesman*, March 16, 1909.

7   **Charting those "vicissitudes":** Reisler, *Great Day in Cooperstown*, 33–34, 49–51, 168–69; Alexander, *Ty Cobb*, 74–75.

8   **Weston got right to it:** "Weston, Walker and Talker," *Yonkers Statesman*, March 16, 1909.

8   **"The effective, moving, vitalizing work":** Hinohara, "History of Medicine."

8   **Osler's speech was big news:** "Medicine: Osler," *Time*, July 13, 1925.

9   **"What [Weston] has done":** "Weston, Walker and Talker," *Yonkers Statesman*, March 16, 1909.

9   **At the same time he was speaking:** "Weston at 71 Starts 4,300-Mile Walk," *New York Times*, March 16, 1909; Wallechinsky, *Complete Book of the Olympics*, 54–55.

11   **In Yonkers Weston spoke:** "Weston, Walker and Talker," *Yonkers Statesman*, March 16, 1909.

11   **Continuing northward through the Westchester County:** Jessica, Arelis, Amberly, Margaretann, "Architecture," *Architecture—Sleepy Hollow & Tarrytown, New York—Then & Now*, Sleepy Hollow Middle School, accessed March 30, 2014, http://www2.lhric.org/pst/shms/tnarch.htm. For more on the election background of Franklin Roosevelt, see "Franklin D. Roosevelt," *Wikipedia*, last modified March 24, 2014, http://en.wikipedia.org/wiki/Franklin_D._Roosevelt.

11   **So Weston's eventful first day:** "Weston at 71 Starts 4,300-Mile Walk," *New York Times*, March 16, 1909; "Weston Retarded by Heavy Roads," *New York Times*, March 17, 1909.

2. "I Fancied I Was a Great Actor"

13   **Edward Payson Weston didn't linger:** "Weston Retarded by Heavy Roads," *New York Times*, March 17, 1909; "Weston Plods Along, Finds Better Roads," *New York Times*, March 18, 1909.

15   **Weston talked quickly:** "Game Old Man Arrived in Reno Last Night," *Reno Evening Gazette*, July 7, 1909; "Weston at Troy, Tells of Bad Roads," *New York Times*, March 19, 1909.

16   **Starting at 6:00 a.m.:** "Weston Plods Along, Finds Better Roads," *New York Times*, March 18, 1909; "Weston at Troy, Tells of Bad Roads," *New York Times*, March 19, 1909.

18   **But Troy was a landmark:** "Weston at Troy, Tells of Bad Roads," *New York Times*, March 19, 1909; "Weston in Mishaps, Pluckily Walks On," *New York Times*, March 20, 1909. For more on the population figures of Troy and the city's baseball background, see "Troy, New York," *Wikipedia*, last modified April 2, 2014, http://en.wikipedia.org/wiki/Troy,_New_York.

18   **Troy's enthusiastic reception:** "Weston in Mishaps, Pluckily Walks On," *New York Times*, March 20, 1909; "Weston 275 Miles on His Long Walk," *New York Times*, March 21, 1909.

19   **It's part of what branded him:** Dave's Vintage Baseball Cards of Los Angeles, http://www.gfg.com/baseball/t218champions.html (web page discontinued).

19   **After resting two hours:** "Weston in Mishaps, Pluckily Walks On," *New York Times*, March 20, 1909; "Weston 275 Miles on His Long Walk," *New York Times*, March 21, 1909.

3. "Pride and Pluck Had Prevailed"

22   **Utica was wild:** "Weston Walks into Fine Condition," *New York Times*, March 22, 1909.

24   **Zigzagging to avoid the ruts:** Nicholson, *Lost Art of Walking*, 70–71; Klinkenborg, "Whirling Sound of Planet Dickens"; Radford, *Celebrated Captain Barclay*.

27   **"I think that I cannot":** Thoreau, *Walking*, 6; see also http://en.wikipedia.org/wiki/Walking_ (Thoreau).

27   **"I, who cannot stay":** Thoreau, *Walking*, 6.

28   **"Go West, young man":** Editor Horace Greeley of the *New York Tribune* is often credited with this famous quote, which was actually made earlier by John B. L. Soule. The quote first appeared as the title to the 1851 *Terre Haute Express* editorial written by Soule. Along with being wrongly credited to Greeley, it has also often been misquoted.

It was originally written as, "Go West, young man, and grow up with the country." Morris, *Lighting Out for the Territory*, 52–53.

28   **Native Americans, he wrote:** Morris, *Lighting Out for the Territory*, 53.

29   **And among the walkers:** Statistics obtained from "Historical Timeline—Farmers and the Land," *Growing a Nation: The Story of American Agriculture*, accessed April 4, 2014, http://www.agclassroom .org/gan/timeline/farmers_land.htm.

29   **In 1883 a man wearing:** DeLuca, *Old Leather Man*, 32; Nicholson, *Lost Art of Walking*, 63–64.

31   **Buried at Sparta Cemetary:** Daily Mail Reporter, "At Last, a Proper 'Burial' for the Mysterious Leatherman, New York and Connecticut's Celebrity Tramp," *Mail Online*, last updated May 26, 2011, http:// www.dailymail.co.uk/news/article-1391004/At-proper-burial -mysterious-Leatherman-New-York-Connecticuts-celebrity-tramp .html.

31   **In 1896 a Norwegian immigrant:** Hunt, *Bold Spirit*.

31   **Weston was neither a tramp nor a fancy:** Marshall, *King of the Peds*, 1–2; Litz, *Montana Frontier*, 2; Weston, *The Pedestrian*, "Memoir" section, 47–48.

32   **That winter, a famous group:** "The Hutchinson Family Singers: America's First Protest Singers," Amaranth Publishing, 2008, accessed April 5, 2014, http://www.amaranthpublishing.com /hutchinson.htm.

32   **Pestering his mother:** Marshall, *King of the Peds*, 1–2.

32   **Silas towered:** Steckel, "History of the Standard of Living in the United States."

33   **A New Hampshire native:** Marshall, *King of the Peds*, 1–2; Litz, *Montana Frontier*, 2.

34   **Years later, Weston related another experience:** "Why Weston Keeps Sunday," *New York Times*, January 18, 1911.

34   **In his teens:** Marshall, *King of the Peds*, 2–10; Litz, *Montana Frontier*, 3.

37   **"It was simply banter":** Weston, *The Pedestrian*.

4. "Undeterred, Undismayed"

39   **And on Sunday:** "Weston Walks into Fine Condition," *New York Times*, March 22, 1909; "Weston Walks in Clay Ankle Deep," *New York Times*, March 24, 1909; "Weston in Blizzard, Halts in His Walk," *New York Times*, March 26, 1909.

39   **"the most hazardous I ever encountered":** "Weston Walks in Clay Ankle Deep," *New York Times*, March 24, 1909.

40 **"that I scarcely remember"**: "Weston Walks in Clay Ankle Deep," *New York Times*, March 24, 1909.

42 **Ducking into the home**: "Weston Walks in Clay Ankle Deep," *New York Times*, March 24, 1909.

43 **What a day that followed!**: "Weston Struggles in Gale and Drifts," *New York Times*, March 27, 1909.

45 **There was a reason**: "Weston Struggles in Gale and Drifts," *New York Times*, March 27, 1909; "Snow Drifts Drive Weston to Fields," *New York Times*, March 29, 1909.

45 **Meanwhile, in southwestern New York**: "Snow Drifts Drive Weston to Fields," *New York Times*, March 29, 1909.

46 **Weston accepted on the spot**: "Snow Drifts Drive Weston to Fields," *New York Times*, March 29, 1909.

46 **An article on Sunday, March 28**: "Is a Grand Old Man," *Syracuse Herald*, March 29, 1909.

47 **The *Times* included its own**: "Snow Drifts Drive Weston to Fields," *New York Times*, March 29, 1909.

48 **"Weston, in spite of his gray hairs"**: "On Foot from New York to San Francisco," *New York Times*, March 28, 1909.

48 **Taking on Dr. Osler's theories**: "On Foot from New York to San Francisco," *New York Times*, March 28, 1909.

49 **"An example to other men"**: "On Foot from New York to San Francisco," *New York Times*, March 28, 1909.

49 **Only Dr. J. Leonard Corning**: "On Foot from New York to San Francisco," *New York Times*, March 28, 1909.

49 **On Monday, March 29**: "Weston at Olean," *New York Times*, March 30, 1909; "Weston Greeted by School Children," *New York Times*, March 31, 1909; "Weston's Last Day in New York State," *New York Times*, April 1, 1909; "Another Transcontinental Walker," *New York Times*, April 2, 1909; "Weston's Auto Lost, Needs His Supplies," *New York Times*, April 3, 1909; "Weston on Worst Roads of His Trip," *New York Times*, April 4, 1909.

49 **"the enthusiasm along my route"**: "Weston Greeted by School Children," *New York Times*, March 31, 1909.

50 **"I . . . thought it best"**: "Weston Greeted by School Children," *New York Times*, March 31, 1909.

50 **At the Reynolds' family farm**: "Weston Greeted by School Children," *New York Times*, March 31, 1909.

51 **"most enthusiastic audience"**: "Weston Greeted by School Children," *New York Times*, March 31, 1909.

51 **"The absence of these necessities"**: "Weston's Last Day in New York State," *New York Times*, April 1, 1909.

52   **Also that Wednesday:** "Another Transcontinental Walker," *New York Times*, April 2, 1909.

5. "I Will Not Alter My Mode of Travel!"

53   **Bounding off the steps:** Marshall, *King of the Peds*, 3–5.
56   **On this trip, Weston would make his way:** http://en.wikipedia.org /wiki/Boston_Post_Road; background on "Trails" from *Road Trails: Early American Roads and Trails* by Beverly Whitaker at http:// freepages.genealogy.rootsweb.ancestory.com/~gentutor/trails .html.
56   **The rubdown in New Brunswick:** Weston, *The Pedestrian*, 21–22; Marshall, *King of the Peds*.
57   **"As I commenced to walk":** Weston, *The Pedestrian*.
58   **Admitting he was "somewhat tired":** Weston, *The Pedestrian*.
58   **"never felt better":** Weston, *The Pedestrian*.
58   **That prompted the president:** Weston, *The Pedestrian*.
59   **"I never have made it":** Weston, *The Pedestrian*.

6. "The People Treat Me Finely"

60   **Preparing to leave:** "Weston's Auto Lost, Needs His Supplies," *New York Times*, April 3, 1909; "Weston Is Cheered by Great Crowds," *New York Times*, April 6, 1909; "Weston Outwalks Johnstown Youth," *New Castle (PA) News*, April 6, 1909.
61   **"I am against these":** "Weston Is Cheered by Great Crowds," *New York Times*, April 6, 1909.
61   **"The . . . miles I walked":** "Weston on Worst Roads of His Trip," *New York Times*, April 4, 1909.
62   **"do much toward keeping":** "St. Yves's Victory Brings Cibot Out," *New York Times*, April 5, 1909, http://query.nytimes.com/mem /archive-free/pdf?res=F10F1FFB3A5512738DDDAC0894DC40 5B898CF1D3.
63   **Canton's city officials were ready:** "Walker Weston Headed This Way," *Massillon (OH) Evening Independent*, April 3, 1909; "Weston Here in a Soaking Rain," *Massillon (OH) Evening Independent*, April 6, 1909; "Weston Is Cheered by Great Crowds," *New York Times*, April 6, 1909; "Weston on Worst Roads of His Trip," *New York Times*, April 4, 1909.
63   **"It is expected that the roads":** "Walker Weston Headed This Way," *Massillon (OH) Evening Independent*, April 3, 1909.
64   **"Not since the days of McKinley":** "Walker Weston Headed This Way," *Massillon (OH) Evening Independent*, April 3, 1909.

65 **"as heavy as lead":** "Weston Here in a Soaking Rain," *Massillon (OH) Evening Independent*, April 6, 1909.

65 **"I tell you, they were":** "Weston Here in a Soaking Rain," *Massillon (OH) Evening Independent*, April 6, 1909.

67 **Decades before Alcoholics Anonymous:** Bellafante, "Lessons on Vice, Liberties and the Law."

67 **Today in New York:** Berger, review of *Island of Vice*.

67 **Detailed in Zack's book:** See Berger, review of *Island of Vice*.

68 **Baseball players were among:** For more on Ed Delahanty, see Sowell, *July 2, 1903*.

68 **Baseball was so saturated with alcohol:** Warrington, *Old Man Booze at Shibe Park/Connie Mack Stadium*.

68 **Weston recognized the dangers:** "Weston on Worst Roads of His Trip," *New York Times*, April 4, 1909.

69 **Weston had stopped in Massillon:** "Weston Here in a Soaking Rain," *Massillon (OH) Evening Independent*, April 6, 1909; "Weston Praises Cletus Wampler," *Massillon (OH) Evening Independent*, April 9, 1909; "Weston Drenched Walking to Wooster," *New York Times*, April 7, 1909.

70 **Wampler was a "bright lad":** "Weston Praises Cletus Wampler," *Massillon (OH) Evening Independent*, April 9, 1909.

71 **It was a gale:** "Weston Buffeted by Fierce Gale," *New York Times*, April 8, 1909.

72 **That was Weston's estimate:** "Mansfield, Ohio," *Wikipedia*, last modified April 9, 2014, http://en.wikipedia.org/wiki/Mansfield, _Ohio; "Weston Buffeted by Fierce Gale," *New York Times*, April 8, 1909; "Weston Talks to School Children," *New York Times*, April 9, 1909; "Weston at Bellevue, Auto Catches Up," *New York Times*, April 10, 1909; "Weston Nearing Chicago on His Walk," *New York Times*, April 11, 1909; "Toledo Welcomes Weston Third Time," *New York Times*, April 12, 1909.

72 **"This is the first real walking day":** "Toledo Welcomes Weston Third Time," *New York Times*, April 12, 1909.

7. "Older Than I Was Twenty-Five Years Ago"

74 **Sunlight streamed:** "Toledo Welcomes Weston Third Time," *New York Times*, April 11, 1909.

75 **"give Americans an opportunity":** "Toledo Welcomes Weston Third Time," *New York Times*, April 11, 1909.

75 **Guggenheim was a car buff:** "M. Robert Guggenheim Held for Exceeding Speed Limit," *New York Times*, June 19, 1909.

75 **At first Ford's Model T:** "Lincoln Highway Photos," *Wyoming Tales and Trails*, accessed April 13, 2014, http://www.wyomingtalesand trails.com/lincoln2.html.

75 **Just a decade before:** *Motor Vehicle Fatalities and Fatality Rates, 1899–2003*, accessed April 13, 2014, http://www.saferoads.org /federal/2004/TrafficFatalities1899-2003.pdf.

76 **Production of the Model T:** Kaszynski, *American Highway*, 26–32.

77 **Stretching west from Toledo:** "Weston Plods Along on Wrong Roads," *New York Times*, April 13, 1909; "Weston Ruffled over Mistakes," *New York Times*, April 14, 1909; "Weston Would Not Sleep in Parlor," *New York Times*, April 16, 1909; "Weston at Hobart, Ind." *New York Times*, April 17, 1909; "Weston Waits for Faster Chauffeur," *New York Times*, April 19, 1909.

77 **"he did not see fit":** "Weston Plods Along on Wrong Roads," *New York Times*, April 13, 1909.

78 **"A chapter of mistakes":** "Weston Ruffled over Mistakes," *New York Times*, April 14, 1909.

79 **"I am inclined to believe":** "Weston Ruffled over Mistakes," *New York Times*, April 14, 1909.

79 **"the best I've seen to date":** "Weston on Good Roads in Indiana," *New York Times*, April 15, 1909.

82 **"It is absolutely necessary":** "Weston off Again; Thanks His Friends," *New York Times*, April 20, 1909.

82 **Even after his first great walk:** Kiczelz, *Weston the Walkist*; Weston, *The Pedestrian*.

84 **"I was always afraid of dogs":** Litz, *Montana Frontier*, 4.

84 **"Being the flamboyant star-of-the-show type":** Litz, *Montana Frontier*, 4–5.

84 **"Probably that is why":** Catton, *Reflections on the Civil War*, 159.

85 **After the Civil War:** Litz, *Montana Frontier*, 4–5.

85 **At some point in the early 1860s:** Litz, *Montana Frontier*, 6; Marshall, *King of the Peds*, 35–40.

85 **"a creature of habit":** Litz, *Montana Frontier*, 7.

85 **"an anxiety-charged atmosphere":** Litz, *Montana Frontier*, 6.

86 **"Forever looking for change":** Litz, *Montana Frontier*, 7.

86 **By the winter of 1866:** Marshall, *King of the Peds*, 11.

86 **"His respectable relatives didn't understand him":** Litz, *Montana Frontier*, 1.

87 **Preparing in 1867 to walk to Chicago:** Marshall, *King of the Peds*, 11.

88 **History doesn't record how many:** Milhollen, *Century of Photographs*, 39.

88   **Using a switch to beat back a crowd:** Marshall, *King of the Peds*, 11–12.

89   **Easy to root for:** Civil War Trust, "Civil War Casualties: The Cost of War; Killed, Wounded, Captured, and Missing," *Civil War Trust*, accessed May 29, 2014, http://www.civilwar.org/education/civil-war -casualties.html.

89   **Weston's first attempt:** Marshall, *King of the Peds*, 9–14.

90   **Some correspondents suggested:** Marshall, *King of the Peds*, 21.

90   **"Clouds of dust and gravel":** Dan Rice, quoted in Marshall, *King of the Peds*, 21.

91   **"I can't do it":** Marshall, *King of the Peds*, 26.

91   **"It was the theater's loss":** Litz, *Montana Frontier*, 1.

91   **A case in point:** Marshall, *King of the Peds*, 25–27.

92   **Apparently, Weston's mother, Marie:** "Why Weston Keeps Sundays," *New York Times*, January 18, 1911.

92   **Nearing the end of his great 1867 trek:** Marshall, *King of the Peds*, 28–34.

93   **"Make your own estimates":** quoted in Marshall, *King of the Peds*, 28–29.

93   **"Gentlemen, I have a short speech":** Marshall, *King of the Peds*, 29.

93   **"Not Grant nor Sherman":** Marshall, *King of the Peds*, 29.

94   **"If any Englishman undertakes":** Marshall, *King of the Peds*, 29.

94   **By doing so, he became part:** Morris, *Lighting Out for the Territory*, 212.

94   **It's no accident:** Chautauqua Institution "Our History," 2013, http:// www.ciweb.org/our-history.

94   **Weston's Opera House lectures:** Marshall, *King of the Peds*, 30–34.

95   **"People argue that because I failed":** Marshall, *King of the Peds*, 30.

95   **"It is possible that if I had been":** Marshall, *King of the Peds*, 32.

95   **"I [did] not know until today":** Marshall, *King of the Peds*, 32.

95   **"Walking as an exercise":** Marshall, *King of the Peds*, 32.

8. "Walking Is the Easiest Part"

98   **A day's walk south of Chicago:** "Weston Tells of His Worry about Help," *New York Times*, April 22, 1909; "Weston Valet Quits; Hunts New Help," *New York Times*, April 23, 1909.

98   **"so slippery one could scarcely keep his feet":** "Weston Valet Quits; Hunts New Help," *New York Times*, April 23, 1909.

98   **"I thought this was a task":** "Weston Valet Quits; Hunts New Help," *New York Times*, April 23, 1909.

99   **"I tell you right now":** "Weston Tells of His Worry about Help," *New York Times*, April 22, 1909.

99   **"I kept the crowd in the rear"**: "Weston Valet Quits; Hunts New Help," *New York Times*, April 23, 1909.

99   **On Thursday, April 22**: "Weston Tells of His Worry about Help," *New York Times*, April 22, 1909; "Weston Valet Quits; Hunts New Help," *New York Times*, April 23, 1909.

100   **A bespectacled, square-jawed man**: "Weston, the Trancontinental Pedestrian," *Reno Evening Gazette*, July 7, 1909; 1890 U.S. Census; "Weston on Worst Roads of His Trip," *New York Times*, April 4, 1909.

100   **How Schinkel was chosen**: "Weston on Worst Roads of His Trip," *New York Times*, April 4, 1909.

100   **Weston said only that they were**: "Weston Falls on Trestle, Hurts Leg," *New York Times*, February 13, 1910.

100   **With Schinkel on board**: "Weston at Bloomington," *New York Times*, April 24, 1909; "Weston's Schedule 68 Miles To-day," *New York Times*, April 26, 1909; "Weston's Big Day," *New York Times*, April 27, 1909; "Weston Walks on Railroad," *New York Times*, April 28, 1909.

101   **"the miles walked equaled"**: "Weston at Bloomington," *New York Times*, April 24, 1909.

101   **"Through all my trip"**: "Weston's Schedule 68 Miles To-day," *New York Times*, April 26, 1909.

102   **"I have not seen anything"**: "Weston's Schedule 68 Miles To-day," *New York Times*, April 26, 1909.

103   **Years later, a reporter who had walked**: "Edward Payson Weston," *Alton (IL) Evening News*, June 10, 1916.

103   **Like a finely tuned Swiss clock**: "Weston Arrested by Negro Officer," *New York Times*, April 29, 1909.

103   **Back in 1871**: For more on the description of the 1871 walk in St. Louis, see "Edward Payson Weston," *Wikipedia*, last modified April 15, 2014, http://en.wikipedia.org/wiki/Edward_Payson_Weston.

103   **Brooklyn, also known as Lovejoy**: Department of Anthropology, University of Illinois at Urbana-Champaign, "Brooklyn, Illinois Archaeology and Heritage Project," *Historical Archeology and Public Engagement*, last modified April 28, 2013, http://www.histarch.illinois .edu/Brooklyn/; "Weston Arrested by Negro Officer," *New York Times*, April 29, 1909; "Weston under Arrest," *New York Times*, April 30, 1909.

104   **"How do I know"**: "Weston Arrested by Negro Officer," *New York Times*, April 29, 1909.

105   **Weston called the roads**: "Weston on Old Trail," *New York Times*, April 30, 1909.

106 **Historians credit its curious name:** Kimball, *Two More Mormon Trails.*

106 **The route was a fresh phase:** "Weston's Stormy Progress," *New York Times*, May 1, 1909; "Weston in Peril on Bridge," *New York Times*, May 5, 1909; "Weston in Hot Sun," *New York Times*, May 6, 1909; "Weston Blown over in Western Gale," *New York Times*, May 2, 1909.

107 **"I experienced a shock":** "Weston in Peril on Bridge," *New York Times*, May 5, 1909.

108 **"We wish you a pleasant trip":** "Weston in Hot Sun," *New York Times*, May 6, 1909.

108 **After the multitude of hardships:** "Weston at Kansas City," *New York Times*, May 7, 1909.

109 **"It does me more good":** "Cheering Throngs Bid Weston Welcome," *Kansas City Journal*, May 7, 1909.

109 **"would have been uncontrollable":** "Cheering Throngs Bid Weston Welcome," *Kansas City Journal*, May 7, 1909.

9. "Make a Good Record First"

111 **By late February 1868:** Marshall, *King of the Peds*, 35–43.

111 **"part of a grand entertainment":** Marshall, *King of the Peds*, 35.

111 **"looking as fresh as a lark":** Marshall, *King of the Peds*, 35.

113 **"The walk was made":** Marshall, *King of the Peds*, 36.

113 **"much annoyed by the sham":** Marshall, *King of the Peds*, 38.

113 **"leaving the pious parson alone":** Marshall, *King of the Peds*, 38.

114 **"die in the attempt":** Marshall, *King of the Peds*, 43.

114 **"Mr. Weston did not seem":** quoted in Marshall, *King of the Peds*, 43.

114 **"Money was an important factor":** Harris, "When Peds Walked the Earth."

115 **Doing so earned him more headlines:** Marshall, *King of the Peds*, 45–46; Harris, "When Peds Walked the Earth"; Wickham, "Edward Weston: The 100K pedestrian"; *Rutland (VT) Herald*, December 28, 2007.

115 **In Rutland, Vermont, a local reporter:** Wickham, "Edward Weston."

115 **Another account had Weston:** Bernstein, "Walking Fever Has Set In."

116 **Weston's status grew:** Marshall, *King of the Peds*, 56–68; Collins, "Old Time Walk and Run."

117 **It was inevitable that Weston:** Marshall, *King of the Peds*, 82–84.

119 **Weston never denied ingesting cocoa:** Karch, *Brief History of Cocaine*, 28–29.

120 **It wasn't long before Weston:** Marshall, *King of the Peds*, 95–125, see especially the poster on p. 95.

120 **"A habit as much as anything else":** Marshall, *King of the Peds*, 125.

121   **"the perfect opposite of Weston"**: Marshall, *King of the Peds*, 112.

121   **The *London Times* described O'Leary's style**: Marshall, *King of the Peds*, 108.

122   **"It was a good week's work"**: Harris, "When Peds Walked the Earth."

122   **One of the ministers that night**: Marshall, *King of the Peds*, 126–31.

123   **O'Leary won that first race**: Marshall, *King of the Peds*, 123, 190.

124   **"all shades of men"**: Marshall, *King of the Peds*, 117, 243–46.

124   **"For the first time"**: Marshall, *King of the Peds*, 247.

125   **"one who has striven to teach"**: Marshall, *King of the Peds*, 247.

125   **"would make all previous efforts"**: "Weston Forced to Change His Route," *New York Times*, June 21, 1909.

125   **Edward Payson Weston had another surprise**: Litz, *Montana Frontier*, 7.

126   **"a bit of a tyrant"**: Litz, *Montana Frontier*, 7.

126   **Many shared the late Henry David Thoreau's passion**: Messent, *Mark Twain and Male Friendship*, 33–34.

126   **"would show their independence"**: Messent, *Mark Twain and Male Friendship*, 33.

127   **"It was as though I had"**: Messent, *Mark Twain and Male Friendship*, 33.

127   **"We have made thirty-five miles"**: Messent, *Mark Twain and Male Friendship*, 34.

127   **"It has long been the custom"**: Messent, *Mark Twain and Male Friendship*, 34.

127   **"Got back to Young's [hotel]"**: Messent, *Mark Twain and Male Friendship*, 34.

10. "Some Command of the Situation"

128   **Folding a map**: "Geographical Center of the United States of America: Lebanon, Kansas," Kansas Travel and Tourism, accessed April 16, 2014, http://www.kansastravel.org/geographicalcenter.htm.

129   **Leaving the Coates Hotel in Kansas City**: "Cheering Throngs Bid Weston Welcome," *Kansas City Journal*, May 8, 1909; "Weston Was Famishing," *New York Times*, May 8, 1909; "Weston Stays in Topeka," *New York Times*, May 10, 1909; "King of Mascots," *New York Times*, May 12, 1909; "Weston Has Mishap," *New York Times*, May 13, 1909; "Weston in Distress," *New York Times*, May 14, 1909.

129   **"so hungry I became faint"**: "Weston Was Famishing," *New York Times*, May 8, 1909.

129 **"He is the best amateur"**: "Weston Was Famishing," *New York Times*, May 8, 1909.

130 **"Reviewing my walk"**: "Weston Stays in Topeka," *New York Times*, May 10, 1909.

131 **"my friends may feel"**: "Weston Stays in Topeka," *New York Times*, May 10, 1909.

132 **For everything that Weston had learned:** "Weston in Distress," *New York Times*, May 14, 1909. For more on the ghost towns of Kansas, see also Amy Bickel, "Black Wolf, Kansas, a Ellsworth County Ghost Town," *Dead Towns of Kansas*, February 4, 2011, http://kansasghost towns.blogspot.com/2011/02/black-wolf-kansas-ellsworth-county .html, and Kathy Weiser and Legends of Kansas, "Black Wolf— Another Farm Town Ghost Town," *Legends of Kansas: History, Tales, and Legends in the Land of Ahs*, March 2011, http:// www.legendsofkansas.com/blackwolf.html.

133 **Black Wolf offered few:** "Weston Covers Up during a Cyclone," *New York Times*, May 16, 1909; "Weston Escorted by Brass Band," *New York Times*, May 17, 1909; "Short Walk for Weston," *New York Times*, May 19, 1909; "Ranchman Rescues Weston from Storm," *New York Times*, May 20, 1909.

133 **"Having fully recovered"**: "Weston Escorted by Brass Band," *New York Times*, May 17, 1909.

133 **"ahead of the time necessary"**: "Weston Escorted by Brass Band," *New York Times*, May 17, 1909.

134 **"My many well-wishers"**: "Weston Escorted by Brass Band," *New York Times*, May 17, 1909.

135 **"If it had not been"**: "Ranchman Rescues Weston from Storm," *New York Times*, May 20, 1909.

135 **Crossing into central Colorado:** "Weston in Lonely Walk," *New York Times*, May 22, 1909; "Weston's Strenuous Week," *New York Times*, May 24, 1909; "Weston near Denver," *New York Times*, May 26, 1909; "Relatives Greet Weston," *New York Times*, May 29, 1909; "Weston in Wyoming," *New York Times*, May 30, 1909.

136 **"came down in torrents"**: "Weston Storm-Bound," *New York Times*, May 21, 1909.

136 **"an occasional rabbit"**: "Weston in Lonely Walk," *New York Times*, May 22, 1909.

136 **"Then I take to thinking of . . . friends"**: "Weston's Strenuous Week," *New York Times*, May 24, 1909.

137 **"Getting my usual daily bath"**: "Weston near Denver," *New York Times*, May 26, 1909.

138 **"Keep away from my heels"**: "Weston at Denver," *New York Times*,
 May 28, 1909.

11. "Shut Up, You Jumping Jack!"

140 **On November 14, 1885**: Marshall, *King of the Peds*, 571, 587–89.

141 **"I haven't walked since March 1884"**: Marshall, *King of the Peds*,
 587.

142 **"Shut up, you jumping jack"**: Marshall, *King of the Peds*, 588.

143 **"Walk out your troubles"**: Roger Tus Love, "Weston the Walkist";
 Van Wert (OH) Daily Bulletin, September 1, 1907; Harris, "When
 Peds Walked the Earth; Wickham, *Edward Weston*.

143 **"Walking," he explained**: Wickham, *Edward Weston*.

143 **There is another reason**: Litz, *Montana Frontier*, 63–64.

144 **In a thinly disguised unpublished short story**: Litz, *Montana Frontier*, 64.

145 **"She didn't steal your husband"**: Litz, *Montana Frontier*, 64.

145 **Back on the roads**: "Big Pedestrian Events Being Planned by Young
 and Weston," *New York Times*, February 28, 1909.

146 **In front of society friends**: Marshall and Harris, "World's Greatest
 Walker."

146 **Leave it to today's experts**: Kravitz, "Age Antidote."

12. "That Awful Strain"

148 **But the prospect of utilizing all that wind**: "Weston in Wyoming,"
 New York Times, May 30, 1909; "Weston Guest at Wyoming Ranch,"
 New York Times, June 2, 1909; "Weston on Lonesome Road," *New
 York Times*, June 4, 1909; "Severe Hardships in Weston's Walks,"
 New York Times, June 6, 1909; "Weston Passes Colorado and Enters
 on Hardest Stage of His Long Walk," *New York Times*, June 6, 1909;
 "A Battle with the Weather" and "Wind Bowls Weston over Embank-
 ment," *New York Times*, June 8, 1909.

149 **Leaving Greeley, Colorado**: "Weston in Wyoming," *New York
 Times*, May 30, 1909.

149 **Quite often I would**: "Game Old Man Arrived in Reno Last Night,"
 Reno Evening Gazette, July 7, 1909.

149 **"the culmination of the most strenuous two weeks"**: "Storms Hold
 Up Weston," *New York Times*, June 1, 1909.

150 **Fortunately, it was a comfortable, spacious place**: For more on the
 history of the Terry Bison Ranch, see Terry Bison Ranch, "About
 Us," *Terry Bison Ranch*, accessed April 17, 2014, http://terrybison
 ranch.com/about.asp.

150 **"a wild, lonesome picture":** "Weston on Lonesome Road," *New York Times*, June 4, 1909.

152 **Weston would be in Wyoming:** "Wind Bowls over Embankment," *New York Times*, June 8, 1909; "Weston without Shoes," *New York Times*, June 13, 1909; "Weston Badly Handicapped," *New York Times*, June 14, 1909; "Weston Laid Up with a Bad Chill," *New York Times*, June 16, 1909; "Weston Recovers Quickly," *New York Times*, June 17, 1909; "Weston Has a Mishap," *New York Times*, June 18, 1909; "Weston Walks at Night," *New York Times*, June 19, 1909; "Railroad to Aid Weston on Road," *New York Times*, June 20, 1909; "Weston Forced to Change His Route," *New York Times*, June 21, 1909; "Weston in the Desert," *New York Times*, June 23, 1909; "Heat Bothers Weston," *New York Times*, June 27, 1909; "Railroaders Help Weston on His Way," *New York Times*, June 28, 1909.

153 **"a magnificent site":** Wyoming State Historic Preservation Office, "Church Butte," *Emigrant Trails throughout Wyoming*, accessed April 17, 2014, http://wyoshpo.state.wy.us/trailsdemo/church_butte .htm.

154 **"all owing to strengthening food":** "Weston in the Desert," *New York Times*, June 23, 1909.

154 **"Notwithstanding all this":** "Weston in the Desert," *New York Times*, June 23, 1909.

155 **"I shall make the best time":** "Railroaders Help Weston on His Way," *New York Times*, June 28, 1909.

155 **The Southern Pacific Railroad Company:** "Railroaders Help Weston on His Way," *New York Times*, June 28, 1909; "Mosquitos Annoy Weston," *New York Times*, June 30, 1909; "Game Old Man Arrived in Reno Last Night," *Reno Evening Gazette*, July 7, 1909; "Mosquitos Like Weston," *New York Times*, July 1, 1909; "Weston Fears Heat in Desert Walk," *New York Times*, July 4, 1909; "Weston in Sandstorm," *New York Times*, July 6, 1909; "Weston at Reno, Nev." *New York Times*, July 7, 1909.

156 **"They came at me":** "Game Old Man Arrived in Reno Last Night," *Reno Evening Gazette*, July 7, 1909.

156 **The first reported use:** Sonenshine and Roe, *Biology of Ticks*, 386.

156 **"The Nevada mosquito":** "Mosquitos Like Weston," *New York Times*, July 1, 1909.

157 **Reno, Nevada, in 1909:** Demers, "London Is not Reno"; "Game Old Man Arrived in Reno Last Night," *Reno Evening Gazette*, July 7, 1909; "Weston in the Sierras," *New York Times*, July 9, 1909; "Hard Strain for Weston," *New York Times*, July 11, 1909.

157 **"swirling seething maelstom":** Edgren, "Battle Mad Mobs Jam Reno."

158 **"I am a few days behind":** "Game Old Man Arrived in Reno Last Night," *Reno Evening Gazette*, July 7, 1909.

159 **"What was your diet in the desert?":** "Game Old Man Arrived in Reno Last Night," *Reno Evening Gazette*, July 7, 1909.

160 **"The air is chilly":** "Weston in the Sierras," *New York Times*, July 9, 1909.

160 To **"realize that":** "Hard Strain for Weston," *New York Times*, July 11, 1909.

161 **"If anyone had told me":** "Weston Laments His Many Mistakes," *New York Times*, July 12, 1909.

162 **Three days remained:** "Weston at End of His Long Streak," *New York Times*, July 15, 1909; "Weston Will Ride Home," *New York Times*, July 18, 1909.

163 **"This company did so much":** "Weston at End of His Long Streak," *New York Times*, July 15, 1909.

164 **"[This] was a great walk":** "Aged Pedestrian Walks 400(0) Miles," *Oakland Tribune*, July 18, 1909.

164 **"San Francisco is not Seattle":** "Weston's Walk," *New York Times*, July 15, 1909.

166 **"It is a big undertaking":** "Weston May Walk Back to New York," *New York Times*, July 16, 1909.

166 **"Meanwhile," said Weston:** "Weston May Walk Back to New York," *New York Times*, July 16, 1909.

166 **It's likely that Weston:** "Weston Returns after Long Walk," *New York Times*, August 16, 1909.

166 **"striving to elevate in popular esteem":** "Weston May Walk Back to New York," *New York Times*, July 16, 1909.

167 **"a demonstration of his easy walking":** "The 39th Annual Meeting," *Fort Wayne Journal-Gazette*, August 13, 1909.

167 **At 4:00 p.m., February 1, 1910:** "Gives Cordial Credentials to Old Friend Weston, about to Walk Again," *New York Times*, January 22, 1910; "Weston to Walk again; Veteran Leaves for Los Angeles Today," *New York Times*, January 24, 2010; "Weston's New Walk Ocean to Ocean," *New York Times*, February 3, 1910; "Weston's Tramp Will End To-day," *New York Times*, May 2, 1910; "Weston Ends Tramp; Welcomed by Mayor," *New York Times*, May 3, 1910.

167 **"strong as a lion":** "Weston's Company Quits," *New York Times*, March 19, 1910.

168 **"the hoodoo," he called it:** "Weston's Tramp Will End To-day," *New York Times*, May 2, 1910.

168   **"I started out on a schedule":** "Weston's Tramp Will End To-day," *New York Times*, May 2, 1910.

168   **"a young old man":** "Weston Ends Tramp; Welcomed by Mayor," *New York Times*, May 3, 1910.

168   **"To drive a good horse":** "Weston's Walk," *New York Times*, May 3, 1910.

168   **Some days later, Weston's friend:** Moler, *Weston and his Walks*, 4.

169   **"attract[ed] more attention":** "The Champion Walker," *Oakland Tribune*, May 16, 1929.

Epilogue

171   **"It was a great walk":** "Weston's Tramp Will End To-day," *New York Times*, May 2, 1910.

171   **New York City's official subway:** "Why Weston Keeps Sundays," *New York Times*, January 18, 1911; see also, Metropolitan Transportation Authority, "New York City Transit—History and Chronology," *MTA.info*, accessed April 18, 2014, http://web.mta.info/nyct/facts /ffhist.htm.

171   **In 1913 the seventy-five-year-old pedestrian:** "Weston's Final Effort," *New York Times*, May 26, 1913; "Weston Ends His Tramp," *New York Times*, August 3, 1913; "Weston to Be a Farmer," *New York Times*, August 29, 1913.

172   **In 1922 the eighty-four-year-old Weston:** "Weston Reaches City Hiking from Buffalo," *New York Times*, October 6, 1922.

172   **By then Weston and Annie O'Hagan:** Vivian Yess Wadlin, "World Class Athlete, Super Star, and Local 'Mystery Man': Edward Payson Weston." *Ulster (NY) About Town.*

172   **Weston could have used the rifle:** "E. P. Weston, 86, Is Shot in Attack on Home; Ulster County Ruffians Beat Pedestrian," *New York Times*, May 17, 1924.

173   **Three days later Weston announced:** "Weston to 'Hit the Trail,'" *New York Times*, May 20, 1924.

173   **However, Weston's only trail:** For more information on Weston's moves, see "Walker Weston Back in City," *Kingston (NY) Daily Freeman*, September 8, 1926; "Anne Nichols Gives $30,000 Fund to Aid E. P. Weston, Aged Walker, Found in Poverty," *New York Times*, March 13, 1927; and "Famous Pedestrian Destitute, Seeks Job," *New York Times*, February 2, 1927.

173   **In 1926 Weston was found disoriented:** "Famous Hiker of Past Only Shadow Now," *Oleon (NY) Evening Times*, June 9, 1926.

173 **Tracked down by a newspaper reporter:** "Famous Pedestrian Destitute, Seeks Job," *New York Times*, February 2, 1927.

173 **But on the day of the newspaper article:** "Aid for Weston, No Job,"
New York Times, February 3, 1927; "Weston Gets Cash and Offer
of a Job," *New York Times*, February 4, 1927; "Anne Nichols Gives
$30,000 Fund to Aid E. P. Weston, Aged Walker, Found in Poverty,"
New York Times, March 13, 1927; "Weston Is Happy on 88th Birthday," *New York Times*, March 16, 1927.

175 **On March 15, 1929:** "Edward P. Weston, 90," *New York Times*, March
16, 1929.

175 **It was Weston's last public appearance:** "E. Payson Weston, Hiker,
Dies at 90," *New York Times*, May 14, 1929.

176 **"Today, most men use their feet":** "The Champion Walker," *Oakland Tribune*, May 16, 1929.

176 **"had been of more cheer":** "His Last Journey," *New York Times*, May
15, 1929.

BIBLIOGRAPHY

Alexander, Charles C. *Ty Cobb*. Oxford: Oxford University Press, 1984.

Bellafante, Ginia. "Lessons on Vice, Liberties and the Law." *New York Times*, March 18, 2012.

Berger, Joseph. Review of *Island of Vice*, by Richard Zack. *New York Times Sunday Book Review*, July 20, 2012.

Bernstein, Walter. "A Walking Fever Has Set In." *Virginia Quarterly Review* 57, no. 4 (Autumn 1980). http://www.vqronline.org/essay /walking-fever-has-set.

Catton, Bruce. *Reflections on the Civil War*. Garden City NY: Doubleday, 1981.

———. *Waiting for the Morning Train: An American Boyhood*. Detroit MI: Wayne State University Press, 1987.

Collins, Kelly. "Old Time Walk and Run." Paper for Ultramarathon Running with Professor Don Davis, Lehigh University, December 11, 1996. http://www.lehigh.edu/~dmd1/kelly.html.

DeLuca, Dan W. *The Old Leather Man: Historical Accounts of a Connecticut and New York Legend*. With editing assistance of and annotation by Dionne Longley. Middletown CT: Wesleyan University Press, 2008.

Demers, Daniel J. "London Is not Reno." *Nevada Magazine*, May/June 2010. http://www.danieldemers.com/NEVADA-MAGAZINE -LONDON-IS-NOT-RENO--STORY-MAY-JUNE-2010.html.

Edgren, Robert. "Battle Mad Mobs Jam Reno," *San Francisco Call*, July 4, 1910.

Harris, Nick. "When Peds Walked the Earth." *Independent*, March 17, 2009. http://www.independent.co.uk/sport/general/athletics/when -peds-walked-the-earth-1646409.html.

Hinohara, Shigeaki. "History of Medicine: Sir William Osler's Philososphy of Death." *Annals of Internal Medicine*, April 15, 1993.

Hunt, Linda Lawrence. *Bold Spirit: Helga Estby's Forgotten Walk across Victorian America.* New York: Anchor Books, 2003.

Karch, Steven B. *A Brief History of Cocaine.* 2nd ed. Boca Raton FL: CRC Press, 2005.

Kaszynski, William. *The American Highway: The History and Culture of the Roads in the United States.* Jefferson NC: McFarland and Company, 2000.

Kiczelz, Paul. "Weston the Walkist: The Making of 'the Pedestrian' (Part 1)." *Walking History.* August 14, 2013. http://walkinghistory.word press.com/2013/08/14/weston-the-walkist-the-making-of-the -pedestrian-part-1/.

Kimball, Stanley B. "Two More Mormon Trails: The Boonslick Trails; The Mississippi Saints' Trail." *Church of Jesus Christ of Latter Day Saints Magazine,* August 1979.

Klinkenborg, Verlyn. "The Whirling Sound of Planet Dickens," *New York Times,* January 15, 2012.

Kravitz, Len. "The Age Antidote." *IDEA Today* 14, no. 2 (1996): 28–35. Online with the University of New Mexico, Albuquerque. http://www .unm.edu/~lkravitz/Article%20folder/age.html.

Litz, Joyce. *The Montana Frontier: One Woman's West.* Albuquerque: University of New Mexico Press, 2004.

Long, H. C. "On the Road with Weston." *Physical Culture* 23 (1910): 580.

Marshall, P. S. *King of the Peds.* Bloomington IN: AuthorHouse, 2008.

Marshall, Paul, and Nick Harris. "The World's Greatest Walker: A Victorian Pioneer of Ultra-marathons (and Coke)." *Sportingintelligence .com,* March 21, 2010. http://www.sportingintelligence.com/2010 /03/21/the-worlds-greatest-walker-ultra-marathons-victorian-pioneer -and-coke-210302/.

Messent, Peter. *Mark Twain and Male Friendship: The Twichell, Howells, and Rogers Friendships.* Oxford: Oxford University Press, 2009.

Milhollen, Hirst D. "Brady-Handy Collection." In *A Century of Photographs, 1846–1946: Selected from the Collection of the Library of Congress,* compiled by Renata V. Shaw, 30–37. Washington DC: Library of Congress, 1980.

Moler, Walter, comp. *Weston and His Walks: Souvenir Programme of the Great Transcontinental Walk, Ocean to Ocean in Ninety Days.* New York: Wynkoop, Hallenbeck, Crawford, 1910. Available online through Library of Congress, https://archive.org/details/westonhis walkssoo00newy.

Morris, Roy, Jr. *Lighting Out for the Territory: How Samuel Clemens Headed West and Became Mark Twain.* New York: Simon and Schuster, 2010.

Nicholson, Geoff. *The Lost Art of Walking: The History, Science, Philosophy, and Literature of Pedestrianism*. New York: Riverhead Books, 2008.

O'Hagan, Conor. "There Was Nothing Pedestrian about One Edward P Weston," *Independent.ie*, April 10, 2014. http://www.independent.ie /lifestyle/health/there-was-nothing-pedestrian-about-one-edward-p -weston-30167283.html.

Radford, Peter. *The Celebrated Captain Barclay: Sport, Gambling and Adventure*. London: Headline, 2001.

Reisler, Jim. *A Great Day in Cooperstown: The Improbable Birth of Base-ball's Hall of Fame*. New York: Carroll and Graf, 2006.

Sonenshine, Daniel E., and R. Michael Roe, eds. *Biology of Ticks*. Vol. 2. 2nd ed. New York: Oxford University Press, 2014.

Sowell, Mike. *July 2, 1903: The Mysterious Death of Hall-of-Famer Big Ed Delahanty*. : MacMillan, 1992.

Steckel, Richard H. "A History of the Standard of Living in the United States." *EH.Net Encyclopedia*, edited by Robert Whaples. July 21, 2002. http://eh.net/encyclopedia/a-history-of-the-standard-of-living -in-the-united-states/.

Thoreau, Henry David. *Walking*. Minneapolis MN: Filiquarian, 2007; origi-nally published in *Atlantic Monthly*, June 1862.

Wallechinsky, David. *The Complete Book of the Olympics*. New York: Little, Brown and Company, 1992.

Warrington, Bob. *Old Man Booze at Shibe Park/Connie Mack Stadium*. Hat-boro PA: Philadelphia Athletics Historical Society. Last modified March 11, 2006. http://philadelphiaathletics.org/old-man-booze-at -shibe-parkconnie-mack-stadium/.

Weston, Edward Payson. *The Pedestrian: Being a Correct Journal of "Inci-dents" on a Walk from the State House, Boston, Mass. to the U.S. Cap-itol, at Washington, D.C. Performed in "Ten Consecutive Days," between February 22nd and March 4th, 1861*. Republished by Ithaca NY: Cornell University Press, 2010; originally published for Edward Payson Weston, 1862.

Whalen, Jim. "Wyoming: An OPEC of Wind Power? Planning Puts State in Good Position." *Wyofile.com*, May 3, 2010. http://wyofile.com/jim_whalen /wyoming-an-opec-of-wind-power-planning-puts-state-in-good-position/.

INDEX

Images are indexed by figure number.